The Picture Man

ARTHUR ERNEST NORTHOVER was born in Northampton in 1924. He enjoyed three entirely different careers – cinema chief projectionist and self-employed mobile cinema showman; advertising manager for the *Northampton Independent*, assistant advertising manager of the *Northamptonshire Evening Telegraph* and a national tyre company; and finally twenty-seven years as proprietor of a fish-and-chip shop, retiring aged 67 in 1990.

He served in the R.A.F. as a squadron electrician on the volunteer reserve list. Before war service he worked in a tannery, a cut-sole factory, a shoe factory, many cinemas, precision engineering, and broke his indentures as an apprentice photogravure printer—after a promising ten months' work—to indulge in his favourite profession, the cinema.

He is a formerly unpublished author, a socialist of the left, a member of the RAF Habbaniya society, and Amnesty International. He was vice-chairman of Rushden & district Music Appreciation society for a number of years, and a member of Rushden & district Cine & Video club.

Marrying Lois Beard Fortescue in 1952, they have reached their Golden Jubilee, and have had three sons and two daughters (the youngest son, Ray, was shot dead at a tragic party in 1986, aged 20).

He is a life-long believer in spiritualism, and follows no church dogma of any description.

Acknowledgements — The author thanks the following for their help and supply of material in compiling this book:

Ken Osborne, Mrs. Pat Turfrey and Mrs. Lesley Wesley (for information about their father, Bob Munn), Mrs. Betty Hancock (sister – for photographs of author and Lois), Neil Dunmore (for photographs of Lings Forum), Kate Taylor (chairman of Mercia Cinema Society), Ian Houseman, and Mervyn Gould.

Every effort has been made to authenticate all information received from these and many others, to whom the author offers his gratitude and apologies for not having mentioned by name.

The Picture Man

Part of a life in Northampton cinemas

Arthur Northover

Mercia Cinema Society

FOR LOIS and our children – WITH LOVE
And in memory of the late Doug Woodford and Bob Munn

Set in 11 point Arial and index compiled by Mervyn Gould. Scan retouching and cover cartoon by Ian Houseman. Printed by Q3 Digital / Litho Loughborough 01509 213456

Published by the MERCIA CINEMA SOCIETY
19 Pinder's Grove Wakefield West Yorkshire WF1 4AH
01924 372748
ISBN: 0 946406 52 9

Contents

Flash-Backs

—"This film and these small photos are pornographic," said a police sergeant. "You'll have to attend court and show a just cause why they should not be destroyed."

—His mother glared at him in temper. "If I ever learn of you rummaging through the dustbins of the Plaza Cinema again for pieces of film, I shall thrash you," she warned.

—The Padre, accompanied by a WAAF officer, after a lengthy preamble, said "You'll be hidden in the metal box you've constructed from wrecked aircraft at the cookhouse cinema for Monday cinema shows. Now, I believe..." The impatient officer interrupted, "It's only a V.D. film! All this fuss Padre. My operator's on leave. It has to be shown. Place something over those peep holes, and ensure my girls cannot see you, airman. Understood?"

—Rolling a thin cigarette carefully between his fingers the Chief Projectionist of the Savoy Cinema paused, and looked at him. "Ah! You! I've heard about you, Wonder boy, who operated a fleapit aged thirteen. Well, this is the ABC, a first class house. Here you'll learn things properly, *the hard way*!" he promised.

—He annoyed a young couple behind him in the cheap seats. "This kid in front keeps looking at us," complained the girl. "Sorry. I'm only watching the projection! They've just changed machines," he replied.

—Peter Sellers sat beside him in a snack-bar: "I'll pretend to drink this coloured piss passed off as coffee. Tell your photographer to take a shot. I'm not keen touring the town shops to advertise my show at the theatre this week. Ugh! Little wonder I feel depressed. Your newspaper gets the cash!"

—"My patient, a boy only eight, has died in the end bed," the night sister told him in the hospital's juvenile ward. "His parents arrived late and argued about a divorce in my office. The very last thing the child enjoyed was your 'Laurel and Hardy' film!"

—A well-dressed matron drew back as I approached her. “Why can’t you buy a ticket yourself’? I do not understand what you say about ‘A’ films. Four-pence is scarcely half the price, since I sit in the shilling seats. Go away, or I’ll call the manager. A boy of your age should not attend a cinema in the evening. It’s disgusting!”

—The Vicar of Silverstone was adamant: “I’m sorry. I cannot permit the Church Hall to be used for a cinema performance during Holy week. Surely you may show two chapters of this *Flash Gordon* serial the following week?”

—Six children staggered into the street coughing, almost falling downstairs from the back-bedroom cinema as his mother stormed at him. “Thank heavens I returned. It's a miracle any one of you are alive. Look at Elsie Harris! Do try to be sick, dear.”

—Fred Irons, chief of the *Ritz* warned him, “It’s only for one day, because the lad is so poorly; but you’ll find working for Charlie at the *Plaza* impossible. He’s a one-man-band, and a weirdo. He’ll not let you touch anything!”

—The sixteen-millimetre projector whined quietly, consuming a huge reel of film in the village hall. In the inky blackness, his hand slowly wandered beneath the dress and along the thigh of a buxom girl. Each week she insisted upon paying for a ticket, despite her gift of a dozen fresh farm eggs!

—At the largest R.A.F. station abroad, Habbaniya, Iraq, the officer in charge of the outdoor and indoor cinemas posed the question. “In addition to your electrical duties on 249 squadron, could you operate the camp cinema? The Group Captain demands a nightly show to ensure morale. Five thousand men - no females. You can train a few bods at a pound weekly, three for yourself.”

—His father-in-law frowned at him. “I sell cars and own a successful garage; an established concern. Do you really believe travelling around villages with a motorcycle combination, showing old films is a business? And with my daughter riding pillion in all weathers? You need to grow up, my lad!”

—On one occasion, he handed a cheque to a bank clerk, who asked him to wait. After a few moments, the manager appeared, cheque in hand.

"This is drawn on the personal account of Major Hereward Wake, the son of Sir Hereward Wake," he declared. "Yes. I arranged a harvest home film show for his tenants at the Courteenhall estate."

"Really! Do you have a bank?"

"Only a Building Society account."

"Indeed! May I suggest we be of service? We handle the capital for the Lord Rank, you know."

—"There must be someone able to sort out the box? That fool set fire to thirty thousand feet of film! The place is in an awful state. It's a wonder the *Picturedrome* wasn't destroyed," pleaded the owner, Harold Pascoe. "Can you help me?"

—"You've broken your indentures, after fourteen months at the printers. The works manager declared you to be the firm's most promising apprentice! 'Photogravure' is a new method - and in seven years' time you could be a qualified tradesman. Look at your friends! Out in the sun these long summer evenings, not shut up in an airless dark room showing pictures," wailed his mother

—A friend, the same age as he, asked, "When I finish work at five, I can view the end product - printed books. By eleven o'clock of an evening what do you find rewarding for all your work? Nothing! And anyway, *no-one knows or cares about you. They all think the manager, who takes all the credit, merely presses a button!"*

—The special Christmas present for 1933, two years prior to the death of his father, was a tin-plate hand-cranked thirty-five millimetre projector: also five small cans containing forty-foot lengths of old film sequences. ***This gift was to change his life completely!***

1: The Cosy Cinema

My outings to the silent cinema with Grandmother were the highlight of any week. From aged four, I can recall many of them vividly. Fortunately, I have an excellent memory. In the 1920s the misnamed *wireless* brought nations together, yet surely as the cinema found its voice, the world discovered this medium infinitely more exciting viewing picture and sound? The atmosphere within a cinema was anything but silent before the innovation of sound. Patrons chattered incessantly on various topics other than the contents of the production.

At The Exchange Cinema, Market Square, Northampton,[1] Frank Slater played accompaniment to silents on the eight-rank Wurlitzer pipe organ.[2] Other cinemas managed with a pianist, while the Picturedrome - built by Charles Robinson, a monumental stonemason, in 1912 - installed a small orchestra, accommodated upon a small balcony, left side of the show, adjacent to the screen. (It is now retained by the Richardson brothers, who operate the premises as a tea-dance venue incorporating large screen video television at the time of writing.)

Sound films, although originally a sensation, were quickly accepted by the public as commonplace.[3] By the mid nineteen-thirties American cinemas introduced double feature shows, sandwiching 'bank night' (bingo) sessions between them in an effort to counteract falling receipts. In Northampton, the Regal, a third rate house, became the first town cinema to offer the double features in 1936.[4]

Until his death in 1935 aged 36, my father suffered tuberculosis through gassing in WW1. He and my mother met me from junior school twice-weekly at 4 pm. We joined a hundred-yard queue at the

---

[1] Converted from a corn exchange to cinema in 1920, by a syndicate of local businessmen. It was bought by P.C.T. in 1928, went to Gaumont-British Picture Corporation. It became the Gaumont, later Odeon /Bingo, and is now the Chicago Hard Rock Café night club.

[2] Slater left G-B. for A.B.C. during WW2, transferring to the ABC Hereford until he retired.

[3] Warner Bros. sound-on-disc Vitaphone process used for The Singing Fool (1928).

[4] The former *Vaudeville*, enlarged in 1930 by John Norfolk, sold to the Southan Morris circuit in 1947 and resold to the Essoldo circuit in 1957 with an appropriate change of name.

Exchange on Mondays, visiting the Cinema de Luxe on Thursdays. I remember Erich von Stroheim in *The Great Gabbo* in 1929 (shown on BBC2 in 1999), also M.G.M's *Love Parade*[5] in which I thoroughly enjoyed the music and spectacle. My mother remarked that Chevalier only became a star because of his accent. Fascinated women were hearing the French language for the first time.

The Desert Song fired the imagination of myself and my school chums. We would leap onto huge piles of sand upon any building site in the neighbourhood, clasping handkerchiefs around our faces, each of us claiming to be the Red Shadow.

The second half of *Wings*[6] amazed patrons when the screen became enlarged for the first wide-screen presentation. Later, on standard-sized screens, the masking was reduced by a hand-turned winch, turned by an operator whenever a sound-on-disc film was shown; picture area being widened when projecting sound-on-film.

A performance at the Exchange always proved to be an evening to remember. From the expensive-looking foyer some thirty steps led to the sixpenny and the shilling seats, pay-box on the right hand side, with a twin pay desk on the opposite flight of stairs. From this level appeared the main foyer, containing an ice-cream bar and chocolate cabin. The twin circle steps on either side of the ground floor led to the front and back circles.

Before entering the sixpennies, which comprised a third of the main floor, we paused, with many other patrons, to view the 'Grotto', a fifteen-foot recess containing a different dramatic or comic work of art advertising the following week's attraction. This depicted a life-like scene from the film using plywood figures of the stars, superbly painted and cleverly lit. Many sequences, from films such as *The Mummy*,[7] or *The Ghoul* starring Karloff,[8] with garishly green and blue under-lit, low lighting, and realistically horrific were the work of Stuart Cook. Mr. Cook joined Gaumont-British from Plymouth in 1933 to produce artistic hand-painted posters for all of the G-B. cinemas in the Midlands. His large studio in the rear of the building accommodated eight full-time artists. The category board items were hand-painted, and if a production were a period piece the wording would be in Old English lettering. Eventually the art works finished at the end of WWII as an economy measure, and

[5] Paramount 1929: Lubitsch
[6] Warners 1929: Robert Florey
[7] Universal 1932: Karl Freunde
[8] G-B. 1933: Michael Balcon

Cook commenced his own sign-writing business, which lasted until his death.

The organ in the Exchange was fixed in the centre of a tiny stage with many pipes visible to left and right of the screen, which was masked with outsize rounded corners, bedecked with one set of tabs (curtains). From the rear seats the large screen appeared very distant, and it was an extremely long throw from the projection room. Here the machines were Gaumont Eclipse, with Western Electric Wide Range sound, and Hall & Connolly arcs using rotating positive carbons to produce perfect burning, but troublesome to maintain!

The interior of the Exchange Cinema in 1920

The brightness produced upon the screen, especially accentuated by the over-lit British films of the thirties, proved to be so hard on the eyes that many patrons joked that sunglasses should be supplied. The footlights were dull amber, without overhead battens; the chief ran the second projector, arc shutter open, slowly moving a frame of coloured gelatines throughout the title and credits of the feature.

A large restaurant/grill-room, operated by Gaumont adjoined the cinema, which included a vast kitchen, baking cakes and bread. During the matinées, afternoon teas were served in the circle during performances. All the circle seats, at one shilling and sixpence and two shillings, were bookable. Performance times, identical with other town cinemas, were 2.30, 6.00 and 8.30 pm. I remember Fox's *Movietone News*, whose trademark, a fluttering Union Jack flag, proclaimed the super-imposed words — *Movietone. It Speaks For Itself.*

In the silent days, lengthy sub-titles consumed almost a third of the news, usually white lettering on a black ground, which strained one's eyes. The organist 'played in' the censor certificate for each short film, as 'interludes' did not commence until the mid-30s. Small cinemas resorted to screen advertising, frequently lasting five minutes. Thankfully, these boring reels were not screened at the Exchange!

The Cosy Cinema

My weekly total of 4½ hours picture-going provided me with an exciting world of reality and make-believe. I'd cut out a viewing panel with a pair of scissors from any card box, and paint scenes from my imagination to slide into the rear, lit by a torch bulb. My parents indulged me by being 'patrons' and peering at my childish presentations, affording them hours of my silence for them to enjoy the wireless. This game resulted in an expensive Christmas present in 1933, a few months before my ninth birthday, at a cost, to them, of ten shillings! I eagerly tore open a large box that contained a tin-plate hand-cranked thirty-five millimetre projector.

The machine, a German 'Bingoscope', some twelve inches high, incorporated a large lamp-house with a door, and inside this, a battery operated lamp. Twin spools, each five inches in diameter, attached to metal arms above and below the gate, were quickly filled with one of the four reels of films supplied. Father made a screen using a piece of plywood. By lunchtime each film had been shown, and the contents were of great interest to my parents. My mother enjoyed a segment from a comedy. "It's Fatty Arbuckle," she cried. "I used to love his two-reelers. Remember seeing this, Ernie, a few years ago?" A piece of *Rookery Nook* followed.[9] "That's Robertson Hare and Ralph Lynn she declared. Before returning to school I had masked the screen with black water-colour paint - another present - and drawn up plans to

[9] G-B. 1930: Tom Walls

make a stage, plus curtains, utilizing cotton and wooden cotton-reels as pulleys.

Two years passed and I studied hard in order to pass my eleven plus exam. An attack of neuritis resulted in a two-month absence and, as a result, I was placed a class down at school. By now the projector had become secondary to my father's deteriorating condition. Cinema visits terminated for them during 1934 and I attended the shows on my own, always visiting the Exchange on Mondays. Here, the supporting short films fascinated me. One of the weekly series - *How To Play Football* - was presented by Ted Drake of Arsenal. The coloured Fitzpatrick travelogues, and the two-reel comedies from 'Radio Pictures', featuring Tom Kennedy and Monte Collins, were hilarious, and did not poach upon the fame of Laurel and Hardy.

I was to enjoy an unforgettable experience at about this time. A ten year-old boy, frequently off school due to a serious illness, had never been to the cinema, and it proved a very exciting experience when I took him to see Jack Hulbert, in *Jack's the Boy.*[10] He possessed no playmates due to prolonged absences, and we were to enjoy only two brief cinema visits. I returned home one tea-time to be informed by my mother that the lad's parents had called, in order to express their thanks for my befriending the boy - who had died during the weekend. So strange, now in my seventies and suffering severe pain after several operations, I frequently see him as clear as yester-year, the thin frame, his short dark hair, and the yellowing complexion always smiling at me. This young boy, whose name I cannot recall, frequently appears within my inward eye.

My parents married in 1922. Purchasing an insurance round for fifty pounds in 1923, my father became the most successful local agent for the company. Gassed in the trenches in 1917, he developed tuberculosis, which ruined a promising career. Unable to cycle because of his condition, he purchased an Austin Seven saloon car and I accompanied him on his rounds on Friday evenings and throughout the Saturdays. On each occasion, I pushed him homewards from the lock-up garage on his cycle, as he freewheeled the half-mile journey. Reduced to barely half a lung, my father died in early 1935. After his death, the mortgage was repaid, and the insurance book sold for £375, leaving Mother financially well-off.

For months the *Bingoscope* projector was forgotten and I tired of the few films.[11] It proved troublesome setting up the machine and

---

[10] G-B. 1932: Walter Forde

[11] The tin-plate railway engines of this factory are now worth c.£2,000. My parents threw the projector away as junk when I was abroad!

screen, drawing the curtains in the summer, for a brief winding of the handle. Relatives did, however, purchase more lengths of film for birthday gifts—usually sequences from sound films containing dialogue with little or no action. Mother reluctantly allowed me to use my bedroom as a cinema. It provided some small recompense for the loss of my father. I have never come to terms with his death, and remember him as a brilliant mathematician and gifted artist.

Digging for treasure

I walked to the nearest cinema to my home, the Plaza (a four hundred and fifty seater with no circle) frequently, counting my pennies to see a second showing of many features previously viewed, years before, in the halcyon days when my parents met me from junior school, such as the Will Hay, Jane Hulbert, and Cicely Courtneidge comedies. They provided nostalgia, laughs, and full houses!

Returning from school during late afternoon, I often pressed an ear to a crack in the rear door of the Plaza and listened to the sound. On one occasion, in the back alley, I noticed several fragments of film on the cobblestones, covered in grit and mud. I realized these must have fallen from the two empty dustbins, so twice weekly I raced from school at lunchtime to raid the bins, searching excitedly through the cigarette ends, sweet wrappers, wet apple cores and orange peelings, all coated with vacuum cleaner dust, my efforts rewarded by finding many lengths and cut frames from damaged films.

Each evening I examined carefully my treasure trove, frames of censor's certificates, and the opening of *Gaumont-British News*, featuring the town crier centre of scene ringing his bell. These bits were swiftly projected as stills onto my screen. *This is the Gaumont-British News, Presenting The World - To The World* I would cry aloud, aping the voice of E.V.G. Emmett. I became fascinated with several pieces where two frames were joined together. How, and Why? Each picture possessed four sprocket holes and one sprocket had been scraped clean, and carefully joined to another?

The science teacher wondered about my sudden interest in the subject, when I enquired about the solvent for celluloid. "Amyl acetate, mixed with some acetone," he explained with a frown. Whenever the original films snapped and broke apart, Dad would have patiently effected a repair, resorting to nail varnish!

Quickly, the bedroom was transformed into a cinema. The screen, with curtains attached, was fixed to the wall at the end of my bed, which provided seating. More remnants of curtain material, fastened to hooks on either wall, partitioned the 'auditorium' from the projection area; two holes were cut for projector lens and my viewing space.

At this time I found I was not content with my old projector and films. A monthly magazine, *Amateur Cine World* had introduced me to sub-standard films, and an array of 16mm. and 9.5mm. projectors were featured. There were, also, articles with photographs depicting 'home cinemas' built in garden sheds and lofts by men with sufficient money to indulge themselves in this new hobby.

Travelling in ladies' hats

Whilst my school chums delivered morning or evening papers, I obtained an easy job delivering ladies' hats for a milliner. My contemporaries were being paid two shillings weekly: I received five shillings for much easier work! Clutching paper bags in each hand, I cycled the area on my deliveries for a mere fifteen minutes after school, Monday to Friday tea-times. The first house I approached presented me with a problem. What should I say? Surely not a crude remark like "Ere's yer 'at, Mrs"?

Instead, I produced a smart hand salute, exclaiming "Dorothea at your service, Madam," and invariably I was requested to wait, and within seconds, the lady would reward me with threepence or sixpence. Each such gratuity was worth an evening at the pictures. The shop owner, Mrs. Burrows, was a wonderful lady in her early fifties, tall, with a nice smile. One day, as I passed through the shop, to a small kitchen for more deliveries, I heard her say in extremely plummy tones, "Oh! It's you, Madam. Just a little tight perhaps? Please allow me to place it on my special stretcher." The way she rolled her r's, when using the word stretcher, reminded me of Martita Hunt, the British actress of countless films.

We met in the rear room, where she dropped her false accent, and said to her partner, "Damn this blasted woman. She's already tried on ten hats!" Sitting down, she placed the hat over one knee and pulled it with both hands. A ripping sound could be heard. "Blast it! I've ripped the bugger! Oh, sorry, dear, shouldn't swear in front of you. There's nothing more to deliver. You can go home - and thanks," she said, breaking off cotton-needle thread with her teeth. Then, making quick repairs, she rose and returned to the front showroom. I followed her, and heard her say, "Madam! My stretcher has improved things a lot - I just know this is you! Oh, yes, absolutely!"

My earnings were not all spent for cinema tickets. I gave two shillings to mother, spent a shilling on myself, and saved the remainder to buy a Pathéscope Ace 9.5mm hand-cranked projector. This 9.5 gauge was ideal, the sprocket holes being centre of the film. A nearby chemist hired films for one shilling per reel per night. His library embraced scores of Chaplin comedies, travelogues, and out-dated silent *Pathé Gazettes*, plus cartoons.

After writing to the publicity people advertising the Isle of Man for holidays, I received several free films, running fifteen minutes each. The advert appeared in the magazine and I felt most mature when I received these spools, addressed to A. E. Northover Esq.

"I wonder what they would say if they discovered a boy of barely eleven played with their films!" remarked my mother.

Running the Cosy

I spent hours producing a poster, which adorned my bedroom wall. Above the doorway, the legend *The Cosy Cinema* appeared inviting, and I was ready for business.

I decided to present a weekly film show for my friends, charging one penny admission. Woolworth's sold a quarter pound of salted peanuts for twopence. These I repacked into smaller bags and sold them for a halfpenny each. This extra income helped to pay for the projector batteries and bulbs, and went towards the hire of a shilling reel. An old gramophone provided music before the shows commenced, and on long strips of discarded blank film I sketched stories of my own, a frame at a time, using water-colour paints revealing them slowly, frame by frame. My *special* feature was 'the walking dead' in *Explosion*, slowly being dismembered by the eruption of a volcano, with my voice-over providing sound effects. These shows lasted roughly forty minutes.

Nearly A Nasty Accident

During a school holiday my mother met a neighbour when shopping. "You'll not be pleased, Florrie, but your Arthur and several other children were climbing all over your freshly decorated bay, entering the house through the window!" My anxious parent hurried home—fortunately for us, otherwise we may all have died. I was busily showing 'second house' after a request from all to see it again and feeling very drowsy. Elsie's brother was sick over my bedspread, and as my mother arrived, she tore down the dividing curtain and flung open the window, shouting for us all to leave at once! Within seconds she was smashing into a lead gas pipe, which I had fractured by using hooks for the curtained division. As she flattened the pipe with a hammer covered by wallpaper, she cried, "Oh, you picture-mad fool! What have I done to deserve this?"

To: Film House
G-B. Picture 172, Wycliffe Rd.
Corporation Northampton
Wardour Street
London

Dear Sirs,
Can I please buy up any of your old junk films for use in my Cosy Cinema? Shilling a reel offered.
Yours sincerely,

Arthur E. Northover

An uncle called during the frenzied activity and eyed the spectacle. "I'll tell you what I think, my dear," he said. "One day, he'll end up running his own cinema!"

I visited a junk shop in town frequently, which sold one hundred foot reels of old cinema film for a shilling each. The eccentrically attired woman who ran it often queried why I extracted film from the centre of the core. I explained, since it was sound film, I was ensuring the conclusion depicted a different scene, and not just dialogue throughout. "You buys 'em in as they are, yer little devil," she snapped.

Among a treasure trove of reels, I possessed a complete trailer for the film *The Lost Squadron*[12] and an action packed sequence of an ammunition dump exploding from *Hells Angels*.[13] I wanted more, but I received no reply to the G-B. letter.

Mother decided the cinema must be closed, to visit her brother in Los Angeles for a six-month stay March 1936. She'd planned to join her brother who had emigrated in 1920, but met my father, fell in love and married. The family, especially my grandmother, thought such a journey a waste of money, though my father wanted mother to use an amount of the life insurance cash after his demise for the trip. Things were made worse by the fact that I refused to accompany her with my four-year-old sister. I had set my heart on attending a certain school - an impossibility if I visited the States. Moreover, the Californian summer vacation lasted for fourteen weeks.

Finally - because she was saving over a hundred pounds on my fare - I was promised a 9.5 Pathéscope 'H' motor-driven projector upon her return.

---

[12] R.K.O. 1932: Selznick
[13] 1930: Howard Hughes

2: Can you take me in, please?

Until the introduction of 'H' (Horrific) certificates in 1938, and 'X' in January 1951, censorship was and remains a farce. Legislation is required urgently to abolish censorship with the exception of 'adult' films, like the removal in 1968 of the Lord Chamberlain's powers over stage performances. Television programmes are uncensored: feature films on video have been checked by a 'classification office'. The Trade self-censors voluntarily, but a situation still exists where a censored, often cut, feature can be banned by over-anxious members of local "watch" committees.

One cold evening, concealed in a shop doorway near the Regal, I waylaid several people without success, asking the usual question: "Excuse me, but if you're going in the cinema would you mind purchasing my ticket, please?" Many officious doormen often created embarrassing scenes for patrons approaching the pay desk: "It's against the law, this sort of thing, you know. I'll permit it just this once." Regular picture-goers accustomed to this practice accepted my money without a word. On this particular night I approached a tall man wearing a large flat cap and grey raincoat to "please take me in, sir". He was most affable.

"I know, sonny. I'll get your ticket. We've missed the shorts. Never mind. I've seen the big picture before. It's terrific. You look cold." I offered a shilling which he refused, saying that he couldn't change the coin. "I shall buy ice-creams. You can pay me afterwards when I've got plenty of change for this ten-shilling note."

The supporting programme was concluding with the news: separate programmes in the 30s. As the feature began I thawed out and quickly became engrossed with *Kind Lady* .[14] After thanking him (he said his name was Herbert) I hurried home to hear the radio before my nine o'clock bed-time. Later, undressing, I found the shilling in my coat pocket and felt mean about this incident.

The 'Tuppenny Rush'

The following Saturday afternoon I queued outside the Regal amid scores of screaming children to join the 'twopenny rush'. Many years were to pass before circuits organised Saturday morning clubs directed by the manager – a.k.a. 'Uncle John' at the Regal. Here, the circle seats cost threepence forming a two-tier social divide, attended chiefly by girls who gazed snootily at the mob below. This *élite* usually

[14] M.G.M. 1935

was infiltrated by many jokers flipping stink bombs below. Apple cores, half-eaten pomegranates, and other fruity objects were hurled back in retaliation. John Norfolk, the proprietor, bellowed for silence, standing beside the ice-cream-stained tabs. "The man upstairs won't start the films until I wave my arms." Hundreds of waving arms! This weekly ritual became part of the fun. After general uproar he always made a different statement shouting himself almost hoarse. "It's possible one of your teachers may be here today!", he raved. Cries of "They wouldn't be seen dead in this dump!." "Shut up!" "We want our money back!". "Start the serial, Baldy!" In unison hundreds of stamping feet, and shrill voices yelling, "We want the serial! We want the serial!"

A tremendous roar deafened everyone as the Universal Studio trade-mark aeroplane circled the globe in silence. A hush descended as the final credit appeared followed by more cheering until the action commenced. *Mystery Squadron* [15] and *Tailspin Tommy* [16] both in twelve episodes more than fired our imaginations. Arguments occurred regarding who might be playing 'Black Ace' in the former – the villain masked by goggles and a microphone covering his face.

Arms outstretched we zoomed along the streets, ladies' hats frequently destined for the gutters as we 'tailspin tommies' passed by: whipping our home-made wooden tops with plaited thongs of leather (remnants from the local shoe factories) caused pain and anger as they caught ladies' legs .... 'boy planes' proved quite a hazard, and pedestrians kept clear of the Regal when we rushed into the streets shouting and screaming.

My form-master posed the question, "Can someone name a famous American other than the President?" "Ray Taylor, sir. He directs all the serials at the Regal."

Thirteen years later my father-in-law mentioned Mr. Norfolk. "I enjoy an occasional drink with him in the Conservative Club. Foolhardy man, Johnny. Spent big money refurbishing the old Vaudeville in Grove Road and renamed it Regal Super Cinema. Fitted out the rear fifteen rows with expensive armchair seats. Put in heavy velour screen curtains, and paid an artist a great deal to produce wall paintings of Venetian scenes. All totally ruined within eighteen months by children's matinées. All for pennies! Called it his cigarette money! No idea whatsoever of business!"

[15] Mascot 1933
[16] Universal 1934

I stayed with my mother's friends Mr. and Mrs. Billington when she sailed for the states in 1936. Here I was allowed to use my bedroom as another Cosy Cinema, though without a curtained section for a box. I affectionately referred to the lady as 'Mrs. B.', who was not impressed with twelve and thirteen year-old boys and girls lying on my bed. Completely naive of sexual mores her warning of "Mind what you get up to, Arthur" mystified me, being absorbed with running the show.

'Mr. B.' worked in the dye department of a local tannery. The palms of his hands were blackened and cracked working with the leathers - apparently they would need years of washing to become normal in appearance. "They are socially sickening. Awful if we are away on holiday – people don't understand. I always wear gloves", he explained. "I like walking, especially when the clocks change. I feel free gloveless striding along in the dark."

On Sunday evenings I learned of other occupational hazards from many people in the local working men's club. Painters suffered lead poisoning, builders were racked with rheumatism, printers complained of upset stomachs, and many shoe workers coughed continually from breathing the dust from soles being stamped out of thick hides. Despite these ailments, with few exceptions, everyone smoked cigarettes and foul-smelling pipes. I attended the club only once. The 'turns' presented on a tiny stage were poor entertainment compared to the cinema.

Ken Green, my closest school friend, and I became regular picture-goers. He had two younger brothers, quite a handful for his parents. His mother was a tall thin unattractive woman with crooked protruding teeth whose lifestyle was a drab drudgery. She washed and ironed clothes for the neighbourhood to supplement her husband's two pounds weekly wages as a railway platelayer. I enjoyed a traditional Sunday lunch of roast beef and Yorkshire pudding, while the Green family often sat down to bread, margarine, and a herring apiece. His parents did not smoke or drink.

* * * * *

All my life I have deplored the great north/south divide. In those hard days of the 30s Mr. Green was working, unlike the thousands of idle men in the distressed areas of Wales and northern England. Fourteen-year old girls were billeted in our area for board and lodging at fifteen shillings a week – paid by the government. Ken and I helped a local policeman going door-to-door collecting unwanted clothing, especially boots for the hunger marchers from the north.

We tried, without success, to understand these bad conditions when viewing newsreels, accompanied by his mother at certificate 'A' films at matinées at the nearby Plaza during school holidays. She introduced us to the glittering musicals of the thirties. Jessie Matthews in *Evergreen,*[17] John Mills singing and dancing in *Car of Dreams,*[18] and *Gold Diggers of 1933* [19] which featured the American 'breadline' in the 'My Forgotten Man' number.

One matinée Ken's mam arranged a party of six children including four girls from the distressed areas to see *Dames.*[20] "I love Dick Powell. These films take me into a world of dreams," she frequently said. Two of the girls were off work with bandaged fingers due to accidents when drilling holes in tiny wheels for toy cars at a local German-owned tin-plate factory. Cheap labour – paid ten shillings for a forty-eight hour week.

The girls sent postal orders for a few shillings home regularly. Becky, from Cardiff, and Stella, from Gateshead, stayed at our house. My mother kept in touch with them for years by mail after they left. Becky died of asthma aged twenty-eight. Stella became pregnant at fifteen, despite my mother's unheeded advice, returned home, married at seventeen, had four more children, and died aged thirty of tuberculosis, in poverty, at Sunderland.

British film-makers never produced one feature depicting life in the thirties. War-time evacuees may entertain albeit with the war background, but *for the thirties*—nothing! Exceptions were Gracie Fields in *Sing As We Go* [21] and others of that genre. Hollywood gave the world *Dead End,*[22] *Grapes of Wrath* [23] and many more. Our studios *finally* released Walter Greenwood's famous play *Love on the Dole* as a feature film in 1941.[24]

Watching *Dames*, Ken nudged me. "Look at my Mam," he whispered. Her expressions were a joy to behold—her lips miming the dialogue, living the characters. Was she Joan Blondell or Ruby Keeler? Somehow she scraped together eighteen pennies to see the film three times during its week's run.

---

[17] G-B.1934/Michael Balcon
[18] G-B. 1933
[19] Warner Bros./Mervyn le Roy
[20] W.B. 1934/Ray Enright
[21] A.T.P. 1934: Michael Balcon
[22] Goldwyn 1937:William Wyler
[23] T.C.F. 1940: John Ford
[24] British National: John Baxter

Ken dreaded leaving school for work; in contrast I could hardly wait to do so. Those afternoons in the Plaza decided my future. I'd become a projectionist, helping to transport the Mrs. Greens *et al.* into a world of make-believe for a few hours, escaping from the reality of a sick society. Could a more rewarding or satisfying job exist?

At the Cinema de Luxe Sammy the one-armed doorman (his other limb left in a Flanders field) would ensure children attended certificate 'A' films: "Do take this lad in—and once inside he can sit anywhere." One Saturday night his help was unnecessary, as I noticed Herbert entering the vestibule. He greeted me explaining that week he had visited ten cinemas, seeing as many features. "This cinema should open for a Friday matinée," he said. Sammy grinned, "One day, perhaps, we will, Mr. Herbert", he said.

I reminded Herbert of the money still outstanding from our last encounter. "Forget it", he said. "I shall pay for you tonight: it's my birthday."

We met twice-weekly for a month throughout the dreadful weather of the summer of 1936. Mother had given me a diary so that she might learn of my activities on her return. My entries merely referred to the weather: "Rain again!" "More rain!" Six months depressing damp conditions prevailed almost daily creating terrible floods throughout much of the country. It was the worst summer of the thirties.

Throughout my mother's and my four-year old sister's six-month stay in California, Mrs. Billington looked after me extremely well. She assumed my frequent references to Herbert were of no consequence, believing he was a schoolboy. Returning from the corner shop one day, she saw me walking down the street with him. Later in the evening she asked if he was a relative. Learning the truth about our association she forbade me to meet him again. Her attitude mystified me. Despite my protests, trying to defend him as 'quite a nice man', she was adamant.

He and I met some days later and I intended to convey her wishes after a cinema visit. We wandered from the Plaza into a park and sat on a bench. My mother sent regularly excellent Hollywood fan magazines, superior to *Picturegoer* and *Picture Show*. I handed Herbert a section from *Hollywood Reporter* containing a list of the cinemas in Los Angeles, which he placed in a leatherette shopping bag. "It's getting dark—I'll read it at home. Let's take a stroll by the river. You can tell me the old film you saw recently *F.P.1.*[25] I missed it years ago."

As we left the park I noticed the gloveless form of Mr. Billington scurrying down a pathway leading to the sunken gardens. "I have to get home by nine: it's quite a journey Herb."

"Not if we walk fast. Warm us up. It's getting chilly: besides, we can see the floods."

We hurried downhill observing the swollen river and flooded meadowland, barely discernible in the fading light. I babbled about the details of a murder mystery, *Hat, Coat and Glove.*[26] "Terrific! Ricardo Cortez. I think he was an old silent star," I enthused.

"I enjoy murders: the best films are murder mysteries!" he replied, gripping my hand. "How about the missing boy who was found in the river just over there by the weir? His head was bashed about. That would make a good murder film. Don't suppose you read the evening paper? Last week, pictures all about it"

I vaguely recalled the Billingtons talking about this, as we approached a just-passable bridge. He raised his voice in order to be heard above the rushing water noisily cascading over a large weir. I shivered. We had faced the wind since leaving the park and the moonlight was frequently obscured by clouds. Wearing open sandals my socks and feet were wet. Miserable and cold I wanted to get home.

I decided to explain Mrs. Billington's objection to our friendship. As I started to speak, Herbert said "I've brought you something to see, more interesting than these film books from America. Special photographs from a French film. Show you them when we reach a street-lamp."

A few sightseers passed by, and then Rushmere Road was deserted. I decided to postpone my important announcement until I reached home, and became engrossed in re-telling the story-line of *F.P.1.* "Fantastic! A floating platform on the ocean. Yet *The Tunnel* [27] was more exciting. Imagine digging a tunnel under the Atlantic. How could anyone build one under this river?" I asked.

"I found a magazine in the park last week full of pictures of fat women—all naked", he said breathlessly. "No need to walk so fast. I don't think it's going to rain!" he said, offering me a Mars bar.

Annoyed with this interruption while recalling the story-line of *The*

---

[25] ('Floating Platform One') G-B. German/French 1932
[26] R.K.O. 1934
[27] G-B. 1934/Michael Balcon

Tunnel in detail, I accidentally knocked the sweet from Herbert's hand. Who cared about fat women in naked photos? Pointless remarks! He sensed my sullen attitude, and referred to the sweet. "Can't see where it's gone. I'll buy another when we reach the corner shops. What's all this about a tunnel?"

I knew you weren't listening to me", I cried loudly, "You were talking about fat ladies."

"Oh that" he said quickly, "I threw the book away into some bushes. "I think you'll like the photos in my bag."

A sandal strap had come loose and I knelt on one knee to secure it. "Can you see the chocolate bar," he asked.

As he spoke I looked up at him. He towered above me; the moonlight caught his bald head. He held his cap in one hand, and the bag swung about in the other: I became extremely frightened. I had never seen Herbert without his cap (usually pulled down to his ears) and his baldness was a revelation. Clearly floodlit by the headlamps of a passing car his strange facial expression scared me as much as a nightmare: staring eyes, with his mouth twisted into a weird smile. His tongue flicked between his teeth like a serpent's. "Let me help you, my dear" he croaked in a strange voice, as he grabbed my right knee, sore and chapped from wet short trousers. I squealed loudly. His face appeared more horrific than Lionel Atwill's in *The Mystery of the Wax Museum*[28] as Glenda Farrell's handbag cracked the wax face in half to reveal the devil beneath.

Screaming loudly, I noticed Mr. B. approaching rapidly. "It's the man I live with," I shouted panic-stricken. "Bloody swine!" exclaimed Herbert, as he ran off into the gloom.

I never saw him again. Was he a child-molester, a murderer, or just a victim of circumstances?

Who can tell?

* * * * * * *

---

[28] W.B. 1933/Henry Blanke

3: A long and winding road

"Can I work in your projection room – please?"

I was in the Regal foyer one Saturday evening in 1937, and addressing John Norfolk, the owner. The small vestibule was packed with patrons—first house had finished, and through the twin doorways spread a double queue which trailed along the street to merge at the single pay-box.

At thirteen years old, five feet three in stature, wearing knee-length trousers, blue jacket, and matching school cap, it was not surprising I was pushed aside by the harassed proprietor.

"Certainly not! Go away."

"Please, I don't want any pay."

"What? Good grief. Wait a moment!"

Ten minutes later I entered a box for the first time. "Suppose you could be useful helping Bailey," Norfolk said as we climbed the two flights of mock-marble stairs leading to the circle. "Here we are," he said, pushing open a door to reveal a rewinding room.

A long wooden bench faced a small frosted-glass window overlooking the street. A hand-cranked rewinder held half a spool of film from a corresponding half spool upon a sturdy metal arm a few inches away: several feet of celluloid dangled to the floor. Barely visible from a heap of damaged lengths of film were two pairs of scissors and a large open bottle of cement. The room reeked of pear drops. Beneath the bench a wooden trestle held ten spools filled with film. Each upright spool was only inches from the floor which, unswept, was covered with sweet wrappers, orange peel, and empty potato crisp packets. I was aware of a rattling projector, and suddenly a young, bespectacled man wearing a grimy brown smock with torn pockets came hurriedly down a flight of concrete steps.

"Ah, Bailey!" Norfolk explained. "This is – what is your name?"

"Arthur."

"Yes. Arthur's going to lend you another pair of hands."

Bailey gave me a swift glance.

"Huh!" he grunted, while muttering 'seventeen, eighteen…' quickly licking a frame of film and scraping off the emulsion with a small penknife, applied cement, and made a splice, counting continuously… 'thirty-four, thirty-five'.

Quickly brushing past us he scampered up the steps as Norfolk said, "Good house. We're almost full. Well, come along, lad, follow me, and see the box."

We ascended the concrete steps, which turned at the top. A large iron door was tied back with cord, and I entered the box: an apt description of a tiny room some seven feet square without a window. Smoke swirled about like early morning mist. Bailey peered over his spectacles into the tiny window of a massive arc-lamp, as I watched with interest. The twin projectors and arc-lamps, much bigger than I had imagined, filled the small room. On the black, shiny spool-box, one word—Kalee. One projector was rapidly consuming celluloid making a loud clicking noise.

Leaving the arc, Bailey opened the door of the top spool box. Pressing the turning spool flanges with the thumb of his left hand he quickly closed the door. He burst into a fit of coughing and selected a wine gum from a roll in his pocket, moving quickly to the idle machine. Pulling several feet of film from the top spool box to the floor he threaded the machine in a few seconds.

"Just burned in some fresh carbons," he managed to say before coughing once more. The pungent smell irritated my throat and I began to cough. The box was hot and airless, with the spool boxes only inches from the ceiling.

"Pack-up night," Norfolk said. "I'll be checking the box office. See you later. Archie here will help you."

On tip-toe I peered through a small glass-covered portal to view a yellow-lit screen which appeared telescopic in reverse. Bailey returned and threaded film to the idle machine and adjusted the carbons. Between this projector and the wall was a space of some eighteen inches, unsuitable for a fat person. Below the portal were a turntable and gramophone records, and a large winding handle which I correctly assumed controlled the tabs. Bailey turned it rapidly with one hand as he pushed a slide upwards on a resistance to fade in the stage lighting with the other. Quickly he switched off the main current to the arc and turning off the motor all was silent, except for the slight sound of a dance band playing 'Smoke Gets In Your Eyes'.

He pushed the specs to his forehead and massaged his eyelids.

"I play one side of a three-minute record, turn it over, and halfway through I fade out, and off we go again: trailers and feature. Gives me a chance to thread up both machines and wind off more reels ready for Percy Higgins. Always run the final reel on its own and rush it downstairs ready for Perce. Film transport. Can't keep him waiting: twelve shows in town as you know, then on to Wellingborough's four, another four from Kettering, and Mrs. Watt's village circuit three, then Luton, and ending up at M.G.M's dump at Rickmansworth. If I'm lucky he'll leave Monday's programme."

"So you can make it up tomorrow?"

"On Sunday! Don't be stupid. I can hold up each reel to the light – like this – see?" With strong light from an overhead light I noticed thick dark slits indicating overlapped joins.

"See them? I spent three hours Thursday morning repairing these old features. So I'll know how much work will be needed on Monday - seat repair day. It's not always hectic like tonight. In a fortnight we've got a six-day booking, so no Wednesday pack-up. Also at matinées we burn these – low intensity carbons." He showed me a thick black carbon rod and a thin one, not copper coated.

"Only require feeding every three minutes. Slow burning. If trade's bad I use them first house. These others – high intensity – burn fast." He moved to an observation port.

"The cinema's clouded with cigarette smoke when full of folk in the evenings. Difficult to cut through the fog of fags. Stand close to the viewing window. It's only cheap glass badly fitted: you can smell the smoke! Oh yes! Don't talk too loud. The place isn't sound-proof. People on the back row can hear."

The performance commenced. Twenty minutes later he changed machines – a hurried complicated procedure. Moving from one projector to the other he lit the arc-lamp on the idle projector, swiftly racing past me to feed the lamp of the operating one. A long cord attached to twin pulleys in the ceiling contained two hooks quickly fixed to the machines. Loud snapping noises could be heard, which I knew were splices crashing through the gate. More banged through on the leader of the other machine after he switched on the motor. A loud snap of the shutters completed the change-over. He rushed beside me, switching off the lamp of the idle machine with the lever of a large wall-switch.

"Hopeless," he exclaimed. "With both arcs on I can scarcely see the screen! It's too much for the generators using high-intensity carbons. Besides, the hall is thick with cigarette and pipe smoke. Take a look."

I gazed into the cinema to view a yellow-coloured screen, covered in scratches, and jump shots with missing action as splices clattered through.

"The old idiot hasn't turned on the extract fans – oh dear!"

He rushed from projector to projector, feeding the arc, moving the carbons with pliers while holding a spool of film beneath his arm. A dangerous practice, I decided, as he dropped the hot carbons with pliers.

"Have to fix this piece in a holder. Carbons are costly."

"Don't you have an assistant?" I asked.

"I've been promised a boy for months. I suppose you'll do. But too young. How much is he paying?" I told him.

"Yes, that's Norfolk for you – and you can have him!"

"I bet you wish you could work at the Savoy!"

"Never!" he snapped. "I hate this place. Bloody awful job. I started as a painter and decorator, gave it up and came here for more money. Two pounds five bob a week – isn't much eh? Norfolk trained me." I frowned. Not much pay for such a great deal of work, I mused, my thoughts interrupted as he continued, "I'm leaving as soon as I find work in a shoe factory. Some of my friends earn almost four pounds a week, and finish at five o'clock. This is a terrible job."

"Well, it's up to you, Arthur. If you want to help, can you come Wednesdays and Saturdays – pack-up nights?"

"Definitely. I can be here by six and stay until nine. On Saturdays all afternoon."

"Now this would be wonderful. Kids' show. Sometimes we run the same programme plus a serial. Often as not it's a different one. Absolute hell! The pictures are almost worn out. Next Wednesday I'll show you how to stick the film together."

"I can do that, it's easy," I assured him. He smiled.

"Yes. I bet you can," he said in disbelief as we returned to the box to show the trailers and reel 1 of *Mama Loves Papa.*[29]

"I've made over four hundred joins in these two features. They're worn out, years old, but Norfolk paid a few pounds for them!"

"He doesn't show a newsreel," I ventured.

"Too costly. Guess what he's planning to do—unbelievable—you've heard of Radio Relay?"

"Yes. My Grandma uses it. Only five shillings a week, and no batteries or wireless needed; just a speaker: the company supply the programme."

"Yes. Relayed from the B.B.C. Norfolk's having this installed free as an advertisement for this firm, to save buying records and paying fees to the Performing Rights people. A wily, mean old boy – Norfolk."

The temperature in the rewinding room seemed like a refrigerator

---

[29] Paramount 1933: Norman Z McLeod

after that of the oven-like box. I shivered as I left the Regal that evening, homeward bound, in the bitter night air. Mother was aghast, learning of this escapade for no pay other than a wine-gum! It had been quite an experience visiting a box for the first time. Many drawbacks I hadn't envisaged. Mending seats! Pasting up posters! One man working alone in terrible conditions! These shortcomings and the poor pay proved puerile in persuading me to leave school for cinema work.

At the Savoy the projection ports numbered nine large portals, and during organ interludes I observed three men busily attending a slide lantern, a spotlight, and a switchboard. The tawdry conditions of the Regal were not evident – the difference between a flea-pit and a first-class cinema!

I worked several evenings weekly at the Regal for almost a year, after delivering ladies' hats, and thoroughly enjoyed operating the box. Bailey went home for three consecutive evenings one week because of a heavy cold which had all the aspects of impending influenza. I carried on alone revelling in every minute, much to the consternation of my parent!

On leaving school, at Easter 1938, I became an indentured apprentice to photogravure printing. I disliked the work and stench of the ink. Also, continually washing-up printing plates and rollers smothered in ink and machine grease did not appeal. The wages were only double the pay of my hat round, at ten shillings weekly, and this didn't help the situation. By mid-summer I smashed a finger between two rubber rollers, and although I was off work throughout July, the evenings still found me in the Regal box. I continued the cinema work often three nights weekly, finding running the box easy apart from pack-ups during the performance Wednesday and Saturday.

Bailey rarely conversed. His training only amounted to the basic principles of projection, supervised by Norfolk, whose technical knowledge was scant. Showing me the batteries under the stage for the Morrison sound system, Bailey added distilled water with what he called 'a squirter.' Explaining that the syringe was known as a hygrometer and used for checking the specific gravity of the acid proved a waste of words. I had learned and handled one at school: the many library books I studied were crammed with interesting data regarding cinemas, yet my knowledge could not be shared with the wine-gum Bailey. Always the same reply – "Who cares? I'll be leaving any day. You can have this silly job."

The printing firm became bankrupt in August 1939. Another company purchased the concern and the staff were given a week's holiday. I never returned.

I longed to find a cinema where I might eventually take over the box. Bailey at the Regal gave me a detailed account of the German equipment at the de Luxe. How one managed to join the staff of the Savoy I could not imagine. The Ritz, Kingsthorpe advertised for 'a willing youth to learn cinema projection'. I seized this opportunity to break my indentures. The management interviewed my mother as I refused to complete my seven-year apprenticeship. Despite mother's tears in the works manager's office, I was adamant, refusing to learn printing in the same stubborn manner I used three years earlier when I preferred not to visit the United States.

* * * * *

For fifteen shillings weekly I met Fred Irons, the chief of the Ritz. He opened the show after ABC closed the Majestic in 1937. A smart, clean box housed Kalee Eleven 'Indomitables', with automatic Kalee arcs and RCA sound, but the uphill cycle ride of three miles from home to the Ritz was a chore in wet weather. The stay at the Ritz, under Fred Irons (former chief of the Majestic, who'd opened the Ritz in 1937) lasted only a week: I left when I learned the Cinema de Luxe was advertising for a youth. Thus within barely a fortnight after escaping from the shackles of the print-shop, I had found a worthwhile future in the picture business.

But whilst I was at the Ritz in 1939, I was sent to help out for one day at the Plaza.

In 1932 the Prince of Wales' Playhouse, empty some time, was refurbished and redecorated as the Plaza Cinema. Charles Lawton, a thick-set five-foot Scot was engaged as operator (projectionist). Local businessmen Messrs. Harris & Faulkner built the Tivoli, Far Cotton; the Ritz, Kingsthorpe; and acquired the Plaza, and ownership of all three eventually passed to the Cipin brothers.

Previously warned about the teetotal, non-smoking Charlie who preferred to work alone, I spent over eight long hours watching this one-man wizard.

"You'll do nuthin', ye understand. Stand an' watch," Charlie instructed when I arrived to relieve the rewind boy – apparently away with 'flu. I could not imagine exactly the duties of the lad. The odour of pear-drops and the acrid stench of new carbons burning in were a peculiar combination. Amyl acetate and acetone bottles stood about the rewind bench, whilst a blue fug of carbon fumes wafted around as a Scottish mist.

Charlie's appearance was odd even for the late 1930s: a large trilby hat with no dent (similar to, but larger than, that worn by Chico Marx), a long black jacket and blue trousers worn 'half-mast' some four inches above a pair of large boots with exceptionally thick soles to enhance his height.

On occasion he ate a meal at the town centre's large 'picture palace' – The Exchange (later Gaumont/Odeon) in the cinema's spacious grill-room restaurant, but his chief friends were the pair of projectors which dwarfed the small Scot!

Fred, chief of the Ritz where I worked on Kalee 11s (Indomitable) and auto high-intensity arcs had told me "Charlie's a weirdo. He has everything arranged in the box to ensure that no-one can operate – only he! Scared of being sacked he keeps a large motor cycle and sidecar outside ready to return to Scotland. Only uses the thing every Friday to tour the town pasting up quad posters."

Film travels through a 35mm. projector at 24 frames per second: even splicing two reels together necessitates changing machines every 20 minutes. The Plaza's out-dated equipment consisted of Gaumont machines and arcs, with antiquated British Acoustic sound, where the film was dragged through a velvet pad. The slightest tear near a sprocket hole would jam, causing a breakdown, accounting for the scores of cut-out frames I found weekly. The carbons required hand feeding every 40 seconds, otherwise a discoloured screen; if they burned too far apart, no picture. Arc fumes at the Ritz were extracted by funnel flues – at the Plaza one constantly breathed the poisonous gases. As he raced between rewinding room and the twin machines, continually counting the seconds to rewind each reel, frequently stopping, re-threading the empty projector, renewing or moving up the carbons while feeding the other arc, Charlie enjoyed roughly one minute's relaxation before changing over machines.

The arc-rectifier room to the right of the box also served for rewinding. The bench with its large handle faced the street, where I frequently watched Charlie winding a large reel. Occasionally he would stop, scissors in hand, holding the celluloid to the light. Over the damaged sprocket holes he delicately welded strips of old film. Operators showing old copies frequently punched holes over the standard dots for changeover purposes at the end of reels; some scratched large crosses, and on films shown for one day – 'Sunday specials' – some resorted to placing a pin through a frame. Obviously, this produced a loud 'snap' as it negotiated the gate skids as a signal for starting the motor of the incoming machine – plus another click indicating changeover. (I found many pieces of old film where the ingenious Charlie had tried unsuccessfully to place tiny celluloid patches over each punch-hole.)

Only a few feet from the bench was the box. The twin Gaumont Chrono projectors each had a raised wooden platform in front of the tiny portholes for Charlie to stand upon due to his height – barely five feet in stature. Since no space existed for a slide lantern (necessary for summoning a patron, usually a doctor, to attend the manager's office), Charlie had constructed an attachment with mirrors and prisms on the side of one arc most effectively. To the right was a non-synch unit (single-turntable record-player). The house lighting and stage flood dimmers were operated from the rear wall of the box, as were the screen tabs.

I was so bored that day – merely watching this busy bee of a man at work yet fascinated with his various actions. He would pull the shutter down for a film ending with a cord in his teeth (run through a pulley attached to the ceiling) as he rapidly closed the screen tabs at the rear wall of the box. (At other shows electrically-operated tabs presented no problem.) The record was quickly faded in as the tabs met: the incoming projector started up within seconds with organ music accompanying the censor's certificate. While the tabs were closed/opened at *speed*, he faded in the stage lighting *slowly* turning by hand a large dimmer. Quite incredible, especially when one considers he was also hand-feeding both arcs.

At the end of the 2.30 matinée I handed him a spool containing 'The King' – a few feet. "Gie it ta' me, ye ken. I have repairs to do. And don't touch things." The day seemed endless watching Charlie showing eleven reels of MGM's *Frou-Frou*, the Gaumont news, and a two-reeler musical *Sometime Soon* – I can still recall the melody some 62 years later.

As I went home at 11 p.m. I looked at Charlie's motor-cycle combination cleaned and polished sufficiently enough for one to eat from, and painted a vivid red (he was colour-blind, incidentally).

He built a rockery garden containing plants and flowers and a water fountain in front of the screen tabs. This played amid coloured lighting frequently spraying water upon the front-row patrons.

Twin 'Girosigns' either side of the entrance used stills from the feature film — hand-coloured behind the photographs and lit intermittently by flashing lamps. These were used in most cinemas throughout the country, but Charlie polished the framed apertures of stainless steel daily, late night, removing any finger-prints by breathing on them and rubbing furiously

Inside the 600-(later 450) seater show the place possessed an odour of its own – due to the frequently-used disinfectant spray containing a pleasing aroma Charlie concocted. He repaired the seats, dispensed with the cleaning ladies, ensuring that everything was scrupulously clean, including the two lavatories. Twice weekly he could be seen atop a ladder changing the canopy letters; each one was constantly re-painted gloss black. In adverse weather conditions every inch of the pavement F.O.H. and some 30 yards from the corner up Monk's Park Road was cleaned of snow and thoroughly salted.

A one-man dynamo whose commutator never became worn or failed!

During the war years I often passed the Plaza on leave at 2a.m. from the midnight Euston train. Charlie could be seen swilling down the pavements with buckets of water, after pasting up several large posters, disdainfully removing the odd cigarette stub. He constantly repainted the interior and exterior of the cinema, and toured the town weekly in a well-polished car to paste up thirty quad posters at various locations.

My mother living nearby was a frequent patron, and never found the presentations lacking in showmanship in any respect. Breakdowns were never known to occur at the Plaza.

For some years in the 50s Charlie *did* have a second. From dozens of rewind boys sacked during Charlie's regime from 1932, John, a stout young man in his late twenties was trained by him, and became a reliable assistant. He was the only other person trusted to operate the Plaza box. So an unusual sight occurred – Charlie outside changing stills while one could hear a projector rattling celluloid though an open window above.

After John's early death, Charlie operated alone again for the rest of his life.

His mother, with whom he lodged, also died, and the bachelor loner moved into the box with a small bed. Housed in the rectifier room, it consisted of a wooden base with a bedroll on top – rolled-up every day in military fashion. Continuous performances became normal procedure; this from 1.45 to 11.00 p.m. on a seven-day week. Charlie worked on alone. A gas ring provided tea and breakfast, with his other meals taken from a next-door café and a near-by fish-and-chip shop. He became obsessed with the place.

In 1969 the Plaza closed, and Charlie was transferred to the ambiguously-named Regal-Plaza Bingo Club at the Grove Road cinema to show afternoon matinées for children. Here, six months later on 19th December, he collapsed in 'the box' thought to be eighty years plus. It was suggested he died of 'a broken heart'.

The Plaza frontage before reconstruction in the 1969s.

The Plaza became the 'House of Holland' store. Twice the staff notified the police after finding goods in disarray on arrival at the store. No intruders had broken in. Thinking the place to be haunted, the female staff refused to use the upstairs lavatories near the former box and preferred to visit the 'Crown and Cushion' pub opposite. The manager of the store, living out of town, stayed overnight on one occasion due to adverse weather. In the early hours he heard a cinema organ playing and Charlie's old mattress moved slowly against the wall.

A poltergeist? The spirit of Charlie? Surely not? I passed by late one evening and thought I saw him behind the rewinding room window, repairing a huge spool of film. In the entry behind the show were fragments of film, yet the Plaza had been closed as a cinema for many years .... however .....

The place was re-built as a TSB bank, which it is still, as Lloyd'sTSB, and staff have not been disturbed since!

* * * * *

The Cinema de Luxe, on a bus route, for a pound weekly, beckoned in the form of the likeable owner Harold Pascoe. "I pay my staff properly, young man," he told me one morning as we met on the top deck of a bus en route to town. "You should meet Harold Aspinal, who operates there. Been with me since 1929 when I bought in the place." I knew the man by sight and quickly made his acquaintance having heard excellent reports of the German projectors in use at Pascoe's two cinemas – the de Luxe and the Picturedrome.

"In 1935 ABC tried buying my show. Always first-run MGM product, you know. Of course they built the Savoy, which reduced my takings for a while, yet I survived", Pascoe explained. "Harold's tired of sacking rewind boys who merely watch films, willing to learn nothing. Give them seven days notice at the Ritz."

Before we left the bus I told him of my ambition to work at the Savoy, and eventually to find work in London. The Stoll Theatre Kingsway appealed to me, as they were engaged in cine-variety. Show places like Paramount's Plaza and M.G.M's Empire, and others in the West End, were the acme of projection perfection – and why not? "May you realise such ambitions. In the meantime you join us, my boy."

In October 1939 I entered the box of Pascoe's de Luxe, and began to learn this profession. Everything to win and nothing to lose! "You seem a sensible lad. If you're willing to learn the technicalities of projection there's a good opportunity here," said Harold Aspinal, the de Luxe's small, wiry chief.

Within a month I was seconded to help a new chief of the 'Drome, Alan Hollis (who came from Luton), as he had no rewind boy, so I worked a week there in 1940. It was at this cinema a few years before where an inept operator threw a reel of burning film from a projector into the rewind room, igniting 20,000 feet of celluloid, which wasn't stored in fireproof containers. Patrons left safely as the fire service swiftly attended. Luckily, the lenses were not cracked and the show reopened after a day and night's closure, now serviced by a retired skilled projectionist, Mr. Munn (father of Bob – see 'Demob Happy'), who'd worked continuously overnight to get the show ready.

Situated on the main Kettering Road, the 'Drome faced the Old

Racecourse, a public park since 1907, with the usual recreational facilities. Referred to as Robinson's, after the man who built it, the 'Drome possessed many obstacles.

The impressive façade had doors at each side leading into a small vestibule with the pay-box. A door on the right led to the box, which was a reasonable size. Here there were Ross front-shutter projectors with Ernemann hand-fed arcs, and Western Electric 'Wide Range' sound. The well-designed low intensity arcs, though hand-fed, gave little trouble, but the mirrors on both were badly pitted and needed replacement, as did the intermittent sprockets on both machines.

The rewind room adjoined the box, and the show was easily run single-handedly. Screen tabs, hand-wound, were used only at the end of the complete performance: regular patrons knew when the films were about to start by noticing the rewind boy walking down the left of the hall and disappearing under the stage to operate the poorly-lit, cheap, thin tabs by tugging the cord hand-over-hand. A tough job, as it ran over several pulleys.

Generators for emergency in the event of a mains failure, housed in a small room adjoining the box, caused chaos. When in use, the noise drowned the sound from the box monitor speaker, and terrific vibration had cracked the ceiling in the vestibule below. Plaster fell upon the pay box! Like the de Luxe, a flat roof outside the box gave fresh air through a curtained doorway. If one stood on the small ladder there, the busy road outside and the racecourse could be seen.

Goodbye, Mr. Chips[30] ran for the week I worked there: it produced good business on its first run in town. Neither cinema operated Friday matinée, but shared a brand-new copy of the *Paramount News.* I cycled between the two three times daily with this.

It was an interesting week, but I was pleased to return to the de Luxe box, where the equipment upstairs matched the posh name. Quiet-running Ernemann projectors with 'Strong' automatic arcs, and Western Electric, an excellent sound system, were installed in both cinemas.

The Chief, Harold Aspinal, had run the de Luxe from 1929, from the introduction of sound. A childless couple, his wife worked as an usherette. Harold's hours, 9.00a.m.-11.00p.m., provided merely Sundays together plus Friday afternoons, when both cinemas dispensed with a matinée. The Guv'nor reduced Harold's pay by a pound weekly, due to poor trade in the summer months.

[30] M.G.M. British 1939: Sam Wood

The Picturedrome at the time of the 40th anniversary in 1952.
From an advertisement in the Northampton Independent.

Incidentally, it is worth recording that only 2d. profit was produced on a one shilling and ninepenny ticket. (8/2d entertainment tax, over 30% film rental plus ten pounds daily for the newsreel with electricity, gas, rates and wages accounts to be paid, also general wear and tear.) The fish and chip shop, adjoining the de Luxe, made 2d. profit on a 'piece and a penn'orth' at 4d.

With only an intake and extractor fans in the ceiling void, the auditorium proved stifling in the summer - the box resembled an oven. Only the Savoy and Exchange shows boasted air-conditioning.

One copy of *Paramount News,* shared thrice daily by both cinemas, was ferried by the rewind boy on a bicycle. One wet night, leaving the 'Drome, I braked fiercely at Clare Street traffic signals, dropping the reel. A ribbon of celluloid unwound down Kettering Road and within seconds, the spool was finally flattened by a Corporation bus.

Harold related stories regarding the nightmare of projection when film sound was introduced. Warner Brothers' Vitaphone process pictures were all sound-on-disc. *The Desert Song* (1930), in twelve eight-minute reels, ran in synchronisation with an equal number of 16" diameter single-sided heavy wax hill-and-dale records running needle-out from centre. Broken fragments of film required blank frames inserted to keep machine and record in 'synch'. Changing projectors every eight minutes, rewinding the spool for the next house, rethreading the idle machine and renewing the carbons, gave a single-handed breathless operator some twenty seconds respite before changing over and repeating the process.

Many operators left the business when sound came in. This was a massive operation, which cost exhibitors a vast amount of money in setting-up new equipment. Sound-on-film was installed as well as Warner's clumsy sound-on-disc system. These discs, played centre-to-edge, were frequently completely out-of-synch. – doors slamming before characters left the screen; a woman's voice as a man was speaking. In addition, sound reproduction was poor: tinny voices accompanied the shrill sound of music. 1929 until late 1930 became a hit-and-miss affair regarding sound films. Harold gave me graphic accounts of the various teething problems. Listening to the many drawbacks involved with early sound films was fascinating, and it was astonishing to me that any projectionists at all stayed in an occupation so fraught with countless technical difficulties.

My brief stay at the Picturedrome made me realise how comfortable projection was at the de Luxe with Harold. The electrically-operated tabs were luxury, despite their slowness, compared with pulling the cord hand-over-hand twice-nightly below the rough stage at the 'Drome.

Hollis returned to Luton. Bernard Burge left the Savoy, where he had been Third, to become the Chief at the 'Drome for Pascoe, thus leaving a position free. Harold recommended me for this.

"You'll be Third at the Savoy. The Chief's son is Fourth, and from what I understand, will shortly get the sack. All he does is watch the films. No interest in the job whatsoever," Harold explained. "Oh, yes," he added, "your pay will be 35/-. Not too bad for beginning, is it? Cut along to the show and meet the Chief during the matinée this afternoon. By the way, I've told him you can make-up the programme, and you're an artist at repairing film. Not that he was convinced. Anyway, see how you get on!"

* * * * *

My first visit to the Savoy proved an unforgettable experience. The assistant manager led the way upstairs to the box. Outside a door carrying the legend STRICTLY NO ADMITTANCE was a large press-button. He pressed this twice. "I'm not sure whether Chief or Doug is on at this time of day".

Doug admitted us. Over six feet tall, with a full head of black tousled hair, he was a commanding figure. I recalled seeing him on previous occasions changing the still photographs in the advertising Girosigns. "Chief will be here soon to relieve me for a tea-break. I'm just near a change-over - won't be a minute. Come on in."

I was astounded at the size of the box, certainly the wrong word to describe the magnificent projection booth, which was at least twenty feet long and over fourteen feet wide. The glowing valves of the Western Electric sound system were against the rear wall. Twin Ross rear-shutter projectors and arcs stood side by side, the cowlings of the flue carriers above them. Both arcs were struck. Beside each machine stood a chair with adjustable foot and back rests. The equipment did not fill the space as in other booths: indeed it appeared dwarfed by the size of the box. On the right was a tall bi-unial lantern, consisting of two small slide lanterns one above the other: each had a small arc with an asbestos curtain at the rear. Next to this was a record reproducer with two turntables, and above a large window into the adjoining rewind room. To the left of the projectors was the Ross spotlight, also arc-fed, facing a large port; the wall beside this housed the switchboard for the stage, display and house lighting.

The walls were neatly tiled in light blue, and the floor was deep brown parquet highly polished. In the middle of the ceiling was a lantern skylight allowing a shaft of sunshine into the place, and everything appeared as clinically clean as though it was an expensive doctor's waiting room. I noticed the Fourth standing beside the spotlight port gazing into the cinema. He paid no heed to my appearance as Doug invited me to stand between the projectors.

"Think you'll like it here?" Doug asked as he switched on the idle machine, without looking into the show. Holding the shutters of both projectors he swiftly pushed them across smartly and tuned off the original machine. No peering into the cinema watching for the standard dots – this changeover was effected in a most nonchalant matter-of-fact manner. He noted my surprise.

"We use paint marks, you know. Come into the rewind room and I'll show you. Wake up Ron! Watch the projector for a moment."

He returned with another spool selected from a long metal storage bin, which was divided into compartments each with a spring-loaded door and holding a double reel of film – not reels standing bare in rows as in the 'flea-pits'.[31] "One Hundred-per-cent fireproof," he pointed out as we returned to the box. On the sprocket holes for the four frames carrying the standard dots were bright yellow paint marks. "Reeves water colour, that's what we use: same for the 'over' frames. No need to look at the screen, these run clearly down the projector. As the final frames go through we switch over. Don't miss a single frame you see. Same for the tab markers at the end of shots, in fact for every film."

As we went to the idle machine he showed the leader to the boy saying "Ninotchka.[32] Parts 5 and 6." This was repeated parrot-fashion by Ron as Doug swiftly threaded-up the machine. "That's a must. Every reel double-checked before threading-up." He adjusted the carbons as he looked into the show.

"Adjust your mirror. The screen's discolouring on the right," he ordered. Seated on the stool beside the arc, Ron winced as he fiddled with a rear control. We moved to the lighting panel as Doug explained it to me. "These switches bring the motors into play. Come with me." In a neat recess outside the box, next to the panel, were several

[31] The film was delivered in 1,000' lengths, doubled during programme make-up to fit on the 2,000' spools used on projectors after sound-on-film came in.

[32] M.G.M. 1939: Ernst Lubitsch. Garbo's last film.

junction boxes and motors. "As you know we have two massive proscenium arches. Between them they contain nearly five thousand lamps. Switch on the motors and the three sets of coloured lamps in each change colours automatically! Very effective during the organ interlude."

An adjoining room housed twenty large batteries. "We turn over to these if the mains lighting fails. Take no chances here I assure you." The next room contained resistances for the arcs with appropriate dials and clapper contacts. I should have known something was missing in the box! Of course, the arc resistances, which always produced heat, and here were outside. At the end was a well-appointed water-closet and wash-hand basin. A first-class hotel could not offer better facilities.

"Let's go back. I can't trust Ron for a minute."

After ordering the boy to rewind the previous reel carefully, Doug seated himself beside the fluttering Ross. He opened the top spoolbox to glance at the rapidly turning spool and check the film time left - not necessary on the Ernemann as a small window was set into the spoolbox door.

"Chief's late. Do you want to wait awhile, or go back to your show?" he asked. "You'll meet him on Monday."

I returned to Harold at the tiny de Luxe box. How small the place appeared after the spacious Savoy booth. Each day for the rest of that week seemed an eternity until the following Monday.

* * * * * * *

4: The ABC / Savoy, Northampton

Northampton's premier cinema, the 1,916-seat Exchange, later Gaumont finally Odeon,[33] had suffered a competitor – the Savoy, Abington Square. Designed by William R. Glen with an imposing façade and built by the local firm Glenn's, it opened with much publicity on Monday 4 May 1936. Although the Compton 3c/7 + Melotone organ elevated 20' from the pit,[34] its mellow tone was no match in sound for the Exchange's stationary-consoled WurliTzer 2/8. The seating capacity was 1,954 -1258 stalls and 696 in the circle.

From the 1936 opening until double-feature shows commenced in early 1938 there were three daily performances: 2.30 - 5.00, 5.30 - 8.00, and 8.30 finishing at 11.00 p.m. All the front circle seats at half-a-crown (2/6d.) were bookable. After each show the entire cinema, including the carpeted rows of seats, was vacuumed. Records played for fifteen minutes, followed by the organ, until the film commenced. Behind the ornate house tabs was a large stage, with the screen tabs open to allow the records to be heard.

The chief was a most experienced electrical engineer, and proved grim as my mentor. Aged 48, he was a Londoner, though he had come to the Savoy from a post in

[33] In The Parade. Now the Chicago Hard Rock Café.

[34] For the organ enthusiast – second-hand from the Princess, Dagenham with 10-tab colour selection. Organ chambers – stage left. Melotone – Series One with glide.

Leamington Spa. He'd been a submariner in WWI, and his frequent phrase "a speck of dust in the torpedo tube was fatal, and grit in the projector gate scratches film" was repetitious, like Granddad's "During the War…" character in *Only Fools and Horses.*

Doug Woodford, who trained at the old Majestic, Gold Street, was transferred as 'second' at the opening.[35]

Chief hand-rolled cigarettes, carefully inserting filter-tips, and could be in a foul mood if the daily ritual went awry. No member of the staff, be it manager, assistant, organist, four male ushers, sixteen usherettes, two page boys, the boiler-man, and four cleaners was allowed in the inner sanctum – the box. Employees rang the exterior bell, or made an appointment to see him, using the internal 'phone system. Moreover, the manager inspected a line-up of the staff in a military fashion fifteen minutes prior to opening for the matinée. Chief would have none of this 'foppery' as he called it.

The manager in my time was Mr. Gregg. Later, I heard that staff lined up for daily inspection chuckled as the pompous opening manager Mr. Pinner addressed them in the circle foyer. Loud guffaws were heard as he issued a warning: "Two members of staff, an usherette and a doorman were in a certain - well (strangulated cough) a certain disgraceful act. On the stairway from the Grand Circle to the car park. Naturally, they are no longer with the company." Among titters he raised his voice. "This sort of practice must cease! To your duties - proceed."

Chief narrowed his eyes, glared at me and from nicotine-stained lips warned, "If I catch you with our elderly sex-pot cashier I shall sack you. She eats little boys under sixteen. We've lost numerous page-boys only fourteen. You know who I mean. Miss Brown!"

After learning such details I paid particular attention to the ample-bosomed lady in question. She repaid my quick glances with a frown of cold indifference. I was now almost seventeen, of course, and appeared older than my age, and so was well past her young-lad date!

Reporting for work at the Savoy, I met Doug and helped him carry a double-feature programme up the six flights of stairs to the rewinding room: quite a chore. Unlike all the other cinemas I knew, this place was warm, being centrally heated. At the de Luxe, making - up the programme with frozen fingers on winter mornings was most

[35] A.B.C. bought this c.1930 and closed it on 26 May 1937 - a year after they opened the Savoy.

difficult; until the matinée began and the arcs and resistances produced heat the cinema was cold. When operating at the 'Drome I put a hand around the side of the arc between reels throughout the afternoon. At the Savoy, the central heating, a constant welcoming warmth kept at a comfortable temperature in every room and passageway, was first class.

Doug made up the programme while I watched, frequently stopping to dampen the sprocket holes over four frames to apply carefully the Reeves yellow water paint. After a while, assuring him of my ability to splice and repair film, I demonstrated using the spare rewinder. He was impressed.

"Nice neat joins. Always use this blooping ink over the sound-track. It avoids sudden plops on the sound. Go over the newsreel and remake any thin lab. joins, they're always very dodgy. I've made-up the show for years. Be my pleasure to hand over to you. See what Chief has to say."

Doug and Chief had worked together since the opening, and held a record of over five years without the slightest hitch or beak in projection. As a film finished, tabs met exactly to the final frame and music crescendo. As the tabs burst open for the next film's certificate not a space of bare screen must be seen. This constituted a breakdown! On the Chief's desk beside the non-synch. turntable a detailed daily log was kept scrupulously: the time and reel number listed, on and off, with the initials of the projectionist on the machine, and who re-wound the reel.

"Chief's red-hot on presentation," Doug told me. "To ensure the sound volume is O.K. from records before the organist takes over, the screen tabs are left open. Never forget to close them. If we ever open up with the main tabs, and the others are open, you'll be sacked. Most important – don't forget what I say."

Each projector was carefully covered in dust-sheets and had lens caps fitted. More sheets engulfed the spot and biunial, and the latter's long, brass, telescopic lens tubes were highly polished, as was the metal-covered wiring to the sound heads. Everything gleamed: spotless, without a fingerprint.

Both pairs of tabs were controlled by push-buttons between the projectors, with red stop buttons to stop at any width for lantern-slide size. During the trailers the slide proclaiming 'All next week' or 'Coming Soon' were superimposed as the trailer appeared.

The entire projection suite adjoined a large verandah encircling the box with fine views of the town and surrounding countryside. One could relax in a deck-chair outside in good weather during tea or supper breaks (on no account were projectionists allowed inside the show).

After this I was taken on a tour of the building. The place was vast, with a great deal of equipment for which the box staff was responsible. Below the operating suite the rectifier room housed two Hewittic mercury arc rectifiers for the arcs.

Through many stairs and passageways we reached the Plenum chamber, which consisted of a huge water-filled tank where to recycle the air extracted it was washed by water-sprays and returned to the cinema. For air brought in from outside, it washed the dust out, too. All this water was a deep brown. [36]

"From nicotine," said Doug. "Rotten job – you'll not like this. Every three months the tank is emptied, and all the interior thoroughly cleaned. The filth builds up and needs to be scraped off. Finally, It's all painted out with red oxide. 'Scraping the bilge', Chief calls it, as he's ex-Navy and 'all bull'."

To the right, next we reached the organ blower motor, and another for powering the organ lift from its deep well to some 15' above the heads of the audience. "There's the boiler room. Place is coke-fired. Come and meet our boilerman." Another motor in here for the automatic stoker!

More motors were situated in a small space behind the ground floor vestibule. This was the central vacuum plant which powered the many suction sockets for the vacuum cleaning hoses.

We left for lunch to return at 1.15.

"Bit different from Pascoe's de Luxe?" Doug asked.

"Formidable!" I exclaimed.

* * * * *

Ron was sacked and before a replacement came along, I found myself sweeping, scrubbing, and vigorously polishing the long box floor as a dreadful weekly task. Chief arrived for a brief hour to relieve Doug for a tea-break. After a two-hour stint I was only half done:

"You can start again –look, boy– grains of sand near the fire buckets".

"I'll get a brush, Chief."

---

[36] Plenum is the opposite of vacuum. As doors were opened, the slightly higher internal pressure would tend to push air out – so eliminating draughts in the auditorium.

"No! You can do it again: sweep, wash and polish Navy style. I've heard all about you wonder-boy who ran a fleapit aged thirteen. The day I can really trust you with this floor will be the time I can safely let you touch a projector."

Morning work (10 a.m. – midday, 9 on Mondays for programme make-up) consisted of servicing the organ lift and blower motors, vacuum plant and replacing dozens of lamps: thousands in the case of the ante-proscenium coves plus those in exit passages and the six lavatories.[37] Each lamp's burning hours was recorded in a logbook, for ABC was careful with money.

The Savoy c.1950. The 3-colour neon-lit ABC name triangle was used by the circuit after the end of wartime lighting restrictions in April 1949. Behind the corner façade can be seen the flat roof of the box. *(Chronicle & Echo)*

One morning Doug and I checked the back-stage dressing-room lamps. In the organist's room I noticed a fan letter and read it aloud: "I get such a thrill when I see your mighty organ rising." "From some fat matron", declared Doug adding, "She'd be lucky, he's a Homo!"

For a few weeks I dreaded Chief entering the box for our daily fifty-minute tea and half-hour supper breaks. Chief used usherettes as spies. He always referred to a small notebook – "Slight rack, Doug, at

---

[37] The inner and outer proscenium coves held a total of c.2,000 lamps.

ten past four." "A browning screen left side at 9.06." "Slight top rack at 4 o'clock; ages before you cleared it." "A slow wipe changeover at 3.33. Was that you Arthur?" I simply nodded. "Not good enough. Buck up." "Tabs opened three feet before censor's certificate appeared on the *March of Time*. In my book this is a breakdown," stormed Chief.

Unlike the present day where videotapes take over after film release, picture-goers who missed a certain production could easily view it on a Sunday show months later. Many renters supplied exhibitors with free programmes for Sundays. Frequently, these copies were in a dreadful state, particularly at the end of reels: blue and white paint marks, punch-holed frames, and scratched crosses, were some of the mutilations. On each splice we used black paint carefully over the sound track to avoid noisy 'plops' from the loudspeakers – we called them 'bloops'.

I attended a council meeting in 1941 where the exhibitors were pressing for Sunday opening. A vicar asked if I wanted to work on the Sabbath. "Absolutely", I replied. "I can enjoy a week-day off and visit the local repertory theatre, or a variety show at the 'Hipp'."[38] Opening was easily granted, as the town was crammed with servicemen including the Anglia Regiment. For us, Sundays were a piece of cake. Two shows – a matinée 2.30-5.00 and one show 6.00-8.30p.m.: usually feature and shorts – no doubles or organ interlude.

Doug Woodford was an extremely good-looking man – broad-shouldered, six feet tall and thick dark wavy hair (which he retained; though greyed, until his death in November 1999, aged 79). He had a winning smile, a Roman nose, and a James Mason profile. Almost all the twenty female staff idolised him without success. I tried dating Joyce, an usherette, who said, "You get me a date with Doug and I'll think about it"!

For organ interludes three operators were required: one on the bi-unial lantern changing slides as the organ pressed the buzzer sounding in the box, another on the dimmer board, also standing by a projector prepared to commence the feature, plus a man on the lime – usually Doug. The lime port was two feet square, and one matinée Doug asked me to take over the lime instantly – "She's there again, Arth." He referred to a beautiful well-attired lady in the rear circle,

---

[38] 'Hipp.' = Hippodrome – a slang term for the elegant New Theatre & Hippodrome (1912) in the town centre seating 2,500 - a cinema in the 1930s with rear projection. Offered to an uncaring council for £10,000 in 1959 who demolished it and later built the Derngate Centre at a cost of millions: still losing money today.

looking over her shoulder and blowing him kisses. I left the lantern for the spot and the frustrated face of this lady is difficult to describe.

The organ interlude was twice daily at 4.10 and 7.10, and she was seated once more waving in the evening only to find me on the lime again. (Incidentally Doug didn't marry until he was 48.)

During the last house sometimes I visited the local fried fish shop for chips and left rewinding until the following morning. Listening to Doug's many experiences here and at the Majestic fascinated me.

Doug Woodford ***(centre)*** **with two army 'mates'.**

One evening on the final screening of the feature I was talking to Doug and complaining about Chief when Doug drew me to the rear of the box. "He can hear every word you're saying. Your voice carries up the open cowling of the arc fume flues. Chief's on the roof." "On the roof? On his day off?" "Yes. Shh! Watching through binoculars – a couple in a bedroom at Overstone Road!"

As time passed, not so many weeks later in fact, Chief was in a foul mood. I asked Doug the reason – "It's the War, isn't it? The black-out! He can't see through the bedroom windows!"

Yes, the war! The 'phoney war' ended and London was being bombed nightly. Newsreels were depicting miserable sequences and the country faced invasion. Whenever the sirens were heard we superimposed a lantern slide over the picture. Trade was excellent, with many service people on leave the matinées were packed with patrons.

After working together for almost six years Doug left for army service (R.E.M.E.), and Frank, directed by the Ministry of Labour, departed to become Chief Engineer at a large local leather tannery. With his salary doubled over that of ABC, he was happy to leave, and in fact never returned to the film business. (Harold Aspinal, of the *de Luxe*, joined British Timken ball-bearings as maintenance engineer.)

Mrs. Wickes in her overalls in 1941 - a hard-working, reliable lady. Photo by the late Doug Woodford.

Suddenly, I became chief overnight.

I began a 100-hour week alone. Yet at only 16, my age contravened the Cinematograph Act. The area service engineer arranged for a middle-aged lady usherette 'bombed out' of her London cinema to assist: officially she was Chief: however, she was God-sent for me, willing to learn and help in any way. She found re-winding painful trying to hold the rapidly-moving film between first finger and thumb to stop and check every splice; instead she steadied reel flanges using a cloth, to keep the film taut. Organ interludes were hectic affairs, yet we coped. I was assured by the management that shortly a replacement chief would be found. Three weeks passed by – sheer hard work!

Mrs. Wickes proved invaluable. I even had her to wash the blue-tiled walls fortnightly, which despite the fume carriers held a thin covering of arc smoke especially from the spot and lantern arcs without flues.

One night during an air-raid, two land mines thudded into the ground, and a series of H. E. (high explosive) bombs rocked the cinema. The whole place seemed to sway slightly. Fortunately, these missed the town's hospital where my mother was undergoing a life-or-death operation, thankfully successful. (The bombs did hit a nearby cemetery, though, rather too gruesome to describe here.) I stood alone by the projector scarcely believing that I was running the entire place, barely six years after operating the toy projector in my back bedroom – 'the Cosy Cinema'.

During the war, everyone was required to join a rota to stay overnight in the cinema for 'fire-watching' duties – merely wander around and be vigilant during air-raids. The first evening I walked around the show, torch in hand, with the cleaners' lights switched on. Flashing the lamp over the seat rows I noticed something shining on the floor behind the rear row of the front circle. It was a two-shilling piece.

Within an excited three minutes I found almost £3 in coins. I raced up the steps to the back row rear circle: another thirty shillings. Treasure-trove indeed! I realised that patrons would rarely, if ever, find a dropped coin which fell silently on the carpet. It occurred to me that more cash must be awaiting collection downstairs under the rear stalls back row. Too true! The total amounted to exactly the pay of the Chief - £4 17s 6d. Other occasions proved less fruitful, just the odd half-crown or sixpence and a few coppers.

Frequently the organist taught a pupil late mornings, and after the learner left the musician would talk a great deal about classical music illustrated by various excerpts of melody. I owe the man a great deal since shortly I commenced attending symphony concerts at the New Theatre, and I've been a devotee since those war-time days.

Southworth opened the place on the organ, followed by Josef Flitcroft, Raymond Charles, and finally Harold Nash, one of the two pianists from the pit of the Repertory Theatre.

One memorable Monday morning I had struggled up five flights of stone stairs with 10 reels of Paramount's *Rhythm on the River* (Crosby's latest),[39] plus the two reels of *March of Time* and *Pathé News,* and an eight reel second feature.

Our new chief: so strange, I cannot recall his name, and so will refer to him as 'Pringle'. He had been 'bombed out' of the ABC Playhouse, Colchester. About five eight, bespectacled, a rather hooked nose, and hair heavily Brylcreemed. He would be in his early 40s, and seemed affable. Not conversant with Ross machines, I left him threading-up at midday, and went home for lunch. When I returned at 1pm for a 1.30 start Mrs. Wickes took me aside to tell me chief apparently had not yet been able to thread-up.

In disbelief I approached him, only to discover he was 'all nerves'. Worse than this, he walked up and down the box like a caged animal muttering about screen lighting and air-conditioning plants. Paramount issued a cue sheet for the Crosby feature: fader no. 8 for this or that

[39] Paramount 1940: Victor Schertzinger.

song; fader no. 6 for Rathbone's dialogue, etc. (Cue sheets were discontinued in the late 30s).

Towards the end of the feature Mrs. Wickes asked me to buy us ice-creams. I left her re-winding and went to the circle 'fridge room. As I came out an usherette hurried down the vomitory steps crying "Arth., there's no picture on the screen!" After running up some twenty-five steps to the box I was met by a distraught Mrs. Wickes. "He's made a mess of the change-over. Switched off the arc of the projector which started showing running-down numbers. Tried to pull the film, before I could stop him, to adjust a large baggy loop – ripped it – oh look!" The projector spewed out a tangled mass of coiled celluloid running onto the floor while the empty machine ticked over, arc still on.

"Kill the arc!", I yelled, "The heat'll crack the condenser lens." As it crunched under his feet, Pringle walked upon the yards of film on the floor to move to the machine. After a few minutes of total chaos the redoubtable Mrs. Wickes carried the concertina-ed pile of tangled film to the re-winding room. I re-carboned a lamp and threaded up a reel. Pringle watched me closely. "Sorry! So sorry!" he said.

The following seven hours were a nightmare. Over thirty splices by hand (we never used a splicer) were made to ensure this reel would run safely next performance. Unfortunately the damage was to one of the Crosby songs.

By the Sunday show, due to commence at 2.30, the programme had not arrived due to air-raids. I decided to show a stand-by feature when Film Transport came. Another nightmare – running 'out-of-the-can'. No time to spool up: each reel placed on a plate in singles, changing over every ten minutes, and hoping that none of the noisy joins clattering through would break.

The only day Mrs. Wickes and I enjoyed was Thursday; Pringle's day off when he toured the country by rail using a Bradshaw making connections here and there: a bachelor and railway buff! After a few weeks of non-stop work and unable to sleep I became ill and spent a few days at home. Another chief, Burgess, arrived, Pringle left, and I was instructed by the Labour Exchange to work in a boot and shoe factory. Later in 1941 Fred Allen became Chief.

Managers Pinner and Gregg were followed by the longest-serving of all – Len Webster, who became one of the best-known public figures in Northampton. He was there for twenty years, retiring as the place was tripled, and had been 'Uncle Len' for thousands of children attending the Saturday morning ABC Minors Club.

Another well-known face belonged to Pat, who ran the foyer sweet kiosk for a long time, and whose face was spot-lit daily with her tray in the ice-cream intervals. When, in the later years of the war, she was 'seconded' to the box, she proved to be a reliable projectionist under Fred Allen.

Twenty years later I was the assistant advertising manager of the Northants. Evening Telegraph, and one evening my wife, Lois, and I visited the Savoy. When we came out late evening and were walking to our car, I heard a shout. It was the old boilerman – I was amazed he was still at the show! "Almost ready for the pension," he said. "I remember you – you ran the show for weeks wartime. Remember that chap Pringle?" I nodded. "You know what happened to him? Just after you left he went somewhere in Herefordshire and topped himself. They found him hanging. Oh, yes! You recall he was bombed out of Colchester? The show suffered a direct hit centre of the auditorium. Full house and he ran off into the street – terrible! Horrible!" And so all those years later I learned how Pringle's nerve failed him in those dark days of the war. The only man to destroy Chief's five-year record – a show without a hitch.

Fred Allen was Chief from 1941, retiring in 1972, and thankfully so missing the place reduced to a triple with cake-stand projection. Unlike all those previous years one man can press three buttons and start a trio of small cinemas. So, all is forgotten – showmanship – three sets of tabs – the innocence of Saturday morning shows. Now the raucous sound – the ads! – padded-out trite two-hour features with four-letter words, D.V.D.... Maybe it will end one day as it began – as a fairground novelty, who can tell?

* * * * * * *

5: Don’tcher Know There’s a War On?

After the Pringle fiasco I ought to have stayed at the Savoy, but the responsibility of keeping this show running with only the help of the redoubtable Mrs. Wickes amid air raids with the inept Pringle underfoot resulted in a near nervous breakdown. Trying to operate during organ interludes running up and down the length of the booth (I cannot term it a ‘box’) from switchboard to hand-fed lantern slide, changing, and arranging coloured gelatines for the lime, proved a twice daily nightmare. Pringle would leave the inner proscenium cove lighting running (using motorised colour changes) into the first reel of the feature if unchecked, and made heavy weather of changing the lime colours – wobbling the spot, upsetting the organist, and creating a distinct feeling of nausea.

Frequently, due to the late arrival of the Sunday programmes, I was obliged to adopt the nerve-wracking practice of running ‘out of the can’; no time for make-up into double reels, changing projectors every ten minutes—no paint cues—relying on standard dots. Worn-out copies for Sundays were packed with buckled over-cemented splices: reels without leaders, only blank film, no numbers, meant changeovers were extremely difficult. The splices clattering through produced ridiculous jump-cuts in action and dialogue. Fade-outs frequently ended a reel, and on the ‘over’, no fade-in. Thus a fresh scene completely ruined continuity. Standing by a projector running worn-out film copies was frightening. A film break *after* it passed through the sound-head was adjusted by allowing film to run on the floor, removing the take-up spool and replace with an empty one, clipping on the film and letting the take-up race to pick up the pile of twisted celluloid from the floor. Conversely a break *before* the sound-head resulted in a shut-down and a re-thread, whilst a full house booed and cat-called. Circuit houses and independents alike suffered their share of bad copies.

Rewinding was a headache: all single reels, re-threading. re-adjusting carbons all within a few minutes, with no competent operator beside the machine one could trust, was frightening. Matinée to commence at two o’clock and the films arriving at one thirty often occurred. A ‘standby programme’ (also in cans as there were not sufficient spools to keep it ready for use on twenty minutes doubles) presented no problem regarding condition having been checked scrupulously for 'V' cuts and splices. One wonders how today's 'operators' using brand-new copies would have coped with these conditions? Plus air-raids and inexperienced staff?

The direction of labour was rigidly enforced during the early days of the war. After the government's panic measure closing cinemas and theatres from 3-9 September 1939, the dark days of 1940 found the industry bereft of skilled technicians. Leaving a situation for another place of work was difficult. A green card was required from the Ministry of Labour before an employee was allowed to engage staff. Cinema projection was considered a 'luxury' trade, and not essential for the 'war effort'.

My projection career in local cinemas from a flea-pit on Kalee 7s to Ross front shutter machines at the Picturedrome, plus the quiet-running Ernemann 5s at the Cinema de Luxe, finished with the all-Ross equipment in the projection booth of ABC's Savoy.

After six months of working in a tannery from 7.30 a.m. to 5 p.m. I arrived home one evening to find Pascoe and Norfolk arguing with each other, both demanding my services to operate their cinemas for a week.

"Seven shillings and sixpence a night, my boy!", offered Norfolk. "Ten shillings!", snapped Pascoe. "He's not helping either of you after working all day", declared Mother.

"Who gave the lad a chance to learn projection?" wailed Norfolk.

"And who never paid him a shilling?" cried Mother.

I decided to operate for Pascoe at the Cinema de Luxe using the auto-arcs and Ernemanns, compared to running up and down stairs at the Regal. Apparently Harold Aspinal was suffering from a bout of influenza, and the programme (*Man in the Iron Mask*[40] + shorts) had been made-up by the operator from the Temperance Hall whose matinées had been cancelled. For a week I cycled three miles to the tannery in the early morning, returning uphill to call at home for sandwiches, cycled to the de Luxe for the 6 p.m. first house, finally closing the tabs at 11 p.m. A long, hard day of fourteen hours!

After a lengthy interview at the Labour Exchange demanding a green card, I returned to the Savoy. A pleasant, likeable, and skilled projectionist by the name of Burgess was Chief. Working with him and Mrs. Wickes, we three enjoyed a worthwhile although short-lived association.

---

[40] U.A. 1939: James Whale

Green cards were not the only reason for the dearth of skilled operators: money proved an important factor. Aspinal left the de Luxe at £4 15s. weekly to become chief electrical maintenance engineer for the British Timson ball-bearing factory at £12 per week. Like-wise his erstwhile beer-drinking companion, the chief of the Savoy, doubled his pay in taking over maintenance work at a large tannery. (It was his departure and Doug Woodford's army conscription happening almost simultaneously which resulted in my sudden promotion to 'chief'—in charge of no-one— as previously described.)

This state of affairs existed for years throughout the industry. Only the circuit houses arranged training facilities to overcome these difficulties. In Audrey Field's book, *Picture Palace,* a photograph depicts a female staff of seven operating the Gaumont, Chadwell Heath in early 1943.

Once again, all was not well at the Savoy. Burgess decided to leave and find a reasonable job with double pay in essential industry. I had volunteered for the Fleet Air Arm without success: a medical examination declared me Grade 2. The Senior Service demanded Grade 1! The drawback was the past medical history of my father—the dreaded word Tuberculosis! This factor dogged my service career. The Navy medical resulted in the doctor saying "...and don't think about sailing under the Red Duster. Or trying for R.A.F. aircrew. The same grade applies!"

Realizing shortly I would join up, hopefully as an electrician, I, too, defected from the box to industry for double pay. 'Second' for ABC paid £3 15s: joining the 25-strong staff of a small engineering factory on a double day-shift (6am - 3pm: 3pm - midnight) earned me £7 weekly. I was engaged on piece-work rates, drilling and tapping holes in tiny aircraft components.

Back in 1940, early on a Sunday morning I was visited by a distraught Norfolk who pleaded for my help. Apparently a disgruntled operator demanding double pay had left without notice the previous evening. The programme was not packed up for Film Transport; moreover, he had sabotaged the equipment in the box. At the Regal, with the operator leaving for Army service, another man decided to sabotage the projection room, after being refused a huge rise in pay. Since the Sunday shows had not yet commenced, I called at Mr. Norfolk's home to collect the keys.

"You'll be the youngest chief in the county", I was assured. A chief,[41] at barely sixteen years old; I could scarcely believe my good fortune, and a good wage.[42]

As I unlocked the place and entered the projection room I was faced with chaos. A large poster was suspended from the ceiling on a piece of string, Daubed on the rear was the message – "Try running this bastard place now, Norfolk! You rotten old tight-wad!"

This character had soaped the projector lenses, the arc condensers, and those of the focusing tubes in the sound-heads. Both arcs were pushed out of alignment. He'd taken brushes from the generators, and removed every light switch in the rewinding room plus four more in the darkened box. By the time I'd rewired the switches and cycled home for my film cement (he'd emptied the entire bottle on the rewinding room floor), it was late afternoon.

I started the generators in the cellar, thankful for the fact that the departing oaf had not put them out of order. Within an hour I realized my ineptitude as a competent projectionist – I'd never been trained to line-up an arc. It was becoming dark outside as, after hours of trial and many errors, I produced a dim flickering picture on the screen. This would never do! In a night sequence nothing could possibly be even slightly discernible with such a poor light source! I worked from 8.00 a.m. until midnight that Sunday, repairing the damage.

Next day, by ten o'clock, I managed to obtain a decently-lit screen, yet it was not correct, since as I fed the carbons the picture was lost in a second unless I used both hands, one to feed the carbons and the other to hold the carbon feeds steady.

The feature *Nurse Edith Cavell*[43] was mutilated, having been projected for the final screening with both gate skates jammed tightly to the film, which had been an almost new copy. The sprocket holes were badly strained and ruined for further exhibition (the renters later presented Norfolk with a £100 bill). I made up the programme, including an old film *Man's Castle*,[44] for the Monday matinée at two o'clock. For that week I was paid £2 for 100 hours. I ran the show

---

[41] It was, and remains, illegal for a person under the age of eighteen to be in full charge of a public cinema projection room.

[42] £2 10s was a derisory pittance. ABC's Frank Heighton was paid £4 15s. and belonged to the Union of Kine Workers. Oddly enough, the Gaumont chief at the Exchange received about £6. Moreover, I hadn't been promised the help of a rewind boy. The unions classed cinemas in four groups alphabetically by takings, size, etc. in relation to wages. The Savoy was A+, the Regal D – the rate here was £3 10s.

[43] 1939: Herbert Wilcox

[44] 1933 Columbia: Frank Borgage

alone for two weeks until a replacement operator was engaged, a fortnight of sheer hell. Apart from the two-level box the Regal possessed many other disadvantages. The generators were housed in the cellar adjoining the gents' toilet, where the main switchboard closely tempted any joker to turn off the supply, plunging the entire cinema into darkness.

From November 1942 to April 1943 I worked in a leather warehouse, operating the Picturedrome on Friday nights giving Bernard a day free (Pascoe never opened for a Friday matinée), for which I was paid 10/-. I volunteered once more for the R.A.F. Bernard Burge left the Picturedrome to become a squadron electrician, and I ceased the Friday night relief job, directed by the Ministry of Labour into an engineering works. Here I graduated to operating a centre lathe, without success, scrapping a great deal of components, a thousandth of an inch too thick or thin, I could not master the lathe or grind a tool, however hard I tried, although I did my best.

In fact the situation had become most embarrassing, since the nine female staff, whose husbands and boyfriends were in the services, jokingly referred to me as 'Scrapper'. Many thought I ruined the metal *in order* to be dismissed and scrap against the Huns or Japs! I felt as ridiculous as Errol Flynn, who with a small group won the war in *Objective Burma* shouting before the final fade-out "O.K. men! Now for a crack at the Japs!" [45]

"I'm letting you go, Northover," snarled the foreman. "You've scrapped so much work it's beyond belief. The army or the coal mines are welcome to you!" It had never occurred to me that the work prevented me from joining the services, and that I was 'screened' by being engaged in an 'essential occupation'.

* * * * * * *

[45] Warner Bros. 1945: Raoul Walsh – taken off after two days at the Warner Leicester Square (Warners' West End showcase) due to public outrage, and not on general release until 1952.

6: Oh, Oh, Oh! What A Lovely War!

So finally, thankfully, 'Scrapper' Northover found himself in the air force. Throughout almost five years' service I spent most of my free time operating cinemas. The Army Kinematograph Unit was a trade, not so in the R.A.F. Here WAAFs, after a few weeks' instruction, used 16mm. machines. They learned how to put a film into a Gebescope upside down, switch on, change a lamp, but nothing more.

At R.A.F. Winfield, serving in an operational squadron of Mosquitos in Scotland 1944, I organised weekly shows in the cookhouse. As we were situated five miles from the Berwick-upon-Tweed cinemas these performances proved most popular. Prior to my arrival at the station a WAAF did her best (with long pauses, switching on the lights while threading up the next reel). She was thankful to hand over presentation to me, especially after opening a reel of *Now Voyager*[46] upside down, carelessly not checking to see if it needed rewinding.

Using wrecked discarded main-plane panels I constructed a box of sorts. Extending a 1600' spool to accommodate over 3,500', I used one projector non-stop, cutting off each spool as shown for return to E.N.S.A. All features shown were new releases. Various farm workers were admitted, at a shilling each, to these weekly shows if space permitted. At times, many stood throughout the two-hour performance, and frequently dozens were turned away. I decided a worthwhile business could be arranged after the war touring isolated villages with a mobile cinema.

The girl was on leave when a V.D. film required exhibition. The W.A.A.F. officer asked me to project, safely concealed in the box. After the twenty-minute documentary featuring diseased female genitals in colour close-up, I removed the film to can it, not realizing that a wooden panel concealing the viewing port had fallen down. Question time suddenly became an uproar of objections to my presence amid much laughter.

"Ma'am, I object. There's a man in there", shouted an indignant woman. "Permission to write to my M.P.? Disgusting!" said another. I became the object of ridicule later at tea-time when queuing for my meal in the cookhouse. The ribald remarks and four-letter words can well be imagined.

---

[46] Warner Bros. 1943: Irving Rapper

In the 30s, the film *Birth of a Baby*[47] was shown to males segregated from females on alternate nights. Later, in the 50s, I was involved with some pornographic pictures received at the local newspaper office when I was advertisement manager of the weekly '*Northampton Independent*'. Alastair Foot, a reporter friend, repeatedly tried to write and produce stage comedies. Finally, based on my experiences, he wrote a full-length play collaborating with Anthony Marriott. The result was to become the longest-running stage comedy in the world, aptly titled: *No Sex, Please, We're British!* Sadly, Alastair died in the wings on the opening night, aged only forty. The piece was later filmed.[48]

After years shut in the box unaware of audience reaction, I found this worthy of study. It is a fact audiences laugh when a dramatic situation is screened: both in the creepy goings-on in the dark of horror films and (due to acute embarrassment) during blatant sex scenes. All the corny *Carry On...*s rely upon lavatory humour. In Paris I was fascinated to view the glittering Italian scene, and the French spectacle when the entire *Folies Bergère Theatre* was lit as stained glass. The British scene consisted of a brothel sequence resulting in belly laughs from British tourists renowned as dirty-minded due to growing up in the repressed society of Britain. Alastair's title was most apt.

During my 18-week course at Hereford, learning aircraft electrics, a radiography unit using 16mm. film concerned the medics., since this X-ray detected a shadow on one of my lungs. After being put to bed in the camp hospital and studied by consultants, who found no trace of shadows or T.B., I was graded 3 for nine months, preventing overseas service.

Every six weeks I was obliged to undergo a chest X-ray. After reporting at the orderly room for details of another chance overseas, I decided to present myself as a malingerer. Standing before the M.O. I said "I'm unfit for service abroad, Sir". Seated at the desk covered with my documents, he frowned impatiently. "Unfit, eh?. Excused marching chit. Excused boots chit. You're one big chit, airman. Your docs. must be as large as the script of *Gone With the Wind*."

I stripped to the waist as he tapped my chest and back. "I'll tell you what I think, you're a first-class scrounger. I detest scroungers." He

---

[47] British 1935
[48] Same title Columbia British: 1973

rolled his r's like Dorothea the milliner. "Cough! and turn your head away. Right. That's it." He returned to the desk, taking up a rubber stamp which he smashed heavily upon a piece of paper – "Approved! Posting approved. Now get out." My ruse had worked.

After technical school I missed a draft to India, thus myself and Bill Mansell, a projectionist who married picture to sound at Merton Park Studios, parted company.[49] We corresponded for a few weeks. He operated the camp cinema at R.A.F. station Chittagong, Karachi.

Three months later I joined 249 Squadron: Mosquitos at R.A.F. Eastleigh, Nairobi.

* * * * *

For almost five months, after combining cinema work with squadron duties, I enjoyed a holiday from projection. Nairobi was a mere ten-minute bus ride from R.A.F. station Eastleigh. A weekly 16mm. film show was presented in the Naafi club rooms given by a young coloured Kenyan. I attended once and after the performance cured a crackle which almost obliterated the sound track from one of the two Gebescope projectors. Contacts rapidly opening and closing under centrifugal force in the motor were dirty: the same trouble had occurred on the well-worn machine in Scotland.

Nairobi boasted two cinemas in 1946: the Capitol and Playhouse. Programmes were of short duration consisting of feature, South African newsreel, and trailers. Personnel were not impressed after years of double-features in the U.K. "Half a show. Picture-goers wouldn't pay to see one film back home," many complained. Strange to discover over fifty years later the identical practice exists throughout Britain for £5 per ticket. Many productions today contain barely 75 minutes of action, all 'padded out' to ensure an average running time of 100 minutes minimum – trailers and ice-cream intervals taking 20 minutes of programme time.

My adventures in East Africa were amusing and numerous and have no place in this book. The vacation from film work was short-lived when the Air Ministry posted the squadron to Iraq. We flew by Dakota via Khartoum and Cairo on 2nd July 1946, six of us plus two aircrew being the holding party. The C.O. gave permission to stay on to thank a British family who befriended myself and associate electrician Taffy Coles (two L.A.C.s who never thought of asking for

---

[49] This small studio is in use for television's 'The Bill' at the time of writing.

promotion to corporal, electrically in charge of twelve aircraft, the well-known verse from 'Bless 'em All' was completely alien to us, being pre-occupied with work).

Nairobi, over six thousand feet above sea-level, provided a superb climate, rarely exceeding 90° in the shade. Constantly passing clouds with sudden rain showers similar to a lovely British summer. Not so R.A.F. Habbaniya in Iraq, fifty miles north of Baghdad. As we landed several men fainted due to the intense heat of over 120° shade. A fierce hot wind burned faces and bare legs like scalding water. Roald Dahl described the place as a hell-hole. Built in the 1930s at a cost of £30m., the station was the largest air force unit abroad. Habbaniya town with the airfield was the third largest and most populated place in Iraq.

The weather conditions were poor, with the shade temperature climbing from 90° May/June to 120°+ by 1 July to the end of August. The centre of the complex was green with eucalyptus and British trees amid much vegetation cleverly irrigated from the near-by Euphrates. Amenities were first-class: many swimming pools, recreational clubs, tennis courts, and horse-riding facilities. Yachting was available on near-by Lake Habbaniya. The churches in the centre (C. of E., O. D., and R. C.) faced two large cinemas; the indoor seating over 1500 including a spacious circle and stage; the outdoor, surrounded by a 10ft brick wall, seated 1,000 patrons on tubular canvas-backed chairs and provided sumptuous picture-going beneath the stars while eating seedless grapes—the acme of luxury. The tiny brick-built box packed with projection equipment at times was 130°+. Prolonged dust storms were frequent all year and the screen subjected to being reduced to shreds by sudden fierce hot gales.

Other air force stations in Iraq were lonely desert outposts with few amenities, usually serviced by 16mm., Shaibah and Kuwait being best described as hell as opposed to Habb. One vital draw-back for personnel was the total lack of female company: men, men, and more men! In the air-conditioned precincts of the hospital were some twenty female nurses rarely observed about camp. Prickly heat rashes spread about wrists and arms rapidly and light loose clothing was worn about the chest impossible for females. Unlike many hot climates the temperature in Iraq after sun-down was only a few degrees lower than day. In the evenings one discarded shorts for full-length trousers, and buttoned-down cuffs. Humidity was extremely high and clothing constantly drenched in perspiration. Squadron working hours were 6–11 a.m. June to mid-August. Four showers daily were necessary, and no-one allowed outside until five o'clock. Heat stroke proved a deadly hazard. I risked this given a special-duty chit to operate the camp cinema a mile away from the barracks.

The chief, an ex-operator at the Paisley Gaumont, a Corporal engine fitter, was 'time X' and returning home.[50] The equipment here was first-class American Super Simplex E7 heads, RCA sound and Strong 'Utility' arcs identical to those proving so trouble-free at Pascoe's de Luxe. Five 'complete changes of programme' weekly. All shows roughly two hours duration which included a serial *The Riders of Death Valley.*[51] *Tailspin Tommy* had been shown, and many others of the *genre*, reminding me of the 'Twopenny rush' matinées. Personnel thought them 'a terrific hoot'. Cinemas in Baghdad ran them frequently, with French sub-titles, all twelve or fifteen chapters at one 4½ hr. sitting, complete with Arabic translation thrown from a slide lantern onto a separate screen. This cinematic creation needed to be seen to be believed. Many films had Arabic / French sub-titles superimposed.

Salman managed broken English and for a few weeks we worked together nicely although his b.o. and sweaty feet were a sickening smell in the confined space of the box of the out-door show. The heat inside the box was unbelievable, with wall resistances identical to the old Regal for the arcs. In such appalling conditions two of my R.A.F. helpers refused to sweat it out, were they paid a small fortune nightly. A mere £1 weekly was no incentive. I worked alone.

I lapsed into nostalgia working this show. Frequently films arrived in jute sacks badly warped by the heat. Many reels had no end tails, nor leaders, just opaque undeveloped film stock with the first number given on sticky paper, or scratched on with a knife or scissors. I remembered films arriving in a sack at the de Luxe many years previously. Pascoe, the guv'nor, gave Harold a fiver to project these special pornographic films at 11 o'clock one Saturday night. Harold offered me a pound to help, if I promised to keep mum about this private show. From mid-morning I worked through the matinée and both evening performances, using a whole bottle of film cement in making at least 400 hand-made splices. All the films were silent, and tinted blue, sepia and amber. Their condition was beyond description in fact as the first reel with strained sprocket holes 'danced' in the

[50] Tour of three years – Time Expired

[51] Universal 1941: Ray Taylor

The cinemas at R.A.F. Habbaniya in July 1946

gate I was obliged to abandon some thousand feet of film as unprojectable.

I retained the hundreds of damaged frames and viewed them later using the old Bingoscope projector from my childhood. Naturally, the many views—in close-up and otherwise—were extremely erotic. One of the naked women was Joan Crawford, who appeared in many 'stag' films in the early 20s. I thought them more pleasing than the real thing.

A part-time usherette who visited the de Luxe box for torch batteries seduced me in the rewinding room. She being in her mid-forties compared to my fifteen years may have accounted for my disappointment. I thought it more romantic and intriguing to be a voyeur than a participant in this act I had heard so much about over the years from school chums, and found over-rated.

How those memories returned in the hot box of the Habbaniya cinema!

The performances were arranged each two days; for example, first house Sunday was shown second house Monday alternating with the other programme. This was repeated Tuesday/Wednesday, Thursday/Friday, and ending on Saturday with two performances of one feature. Thus there were seven programmes to make up, much winding and rewinding, and little if any time to watch more than a minute of film. Arranging extra staff to train was difficult due to bods on leave (cooling down for a week in Cyprus or Cairo, at only 90° in the shade), or suddenly going home as their 'demob. numbers' came up.[52]

One assistant stayed with me for eight months, Corporal Cooper, a rigger attached to the servicing unit of Transport Command. Unfortunately, the C. of E. padre arranged a compassionate home posting for 'Coop' after his wife sent him a 'Dear John' letter: Due for de-mob. within a few months, the Padre said "Turn up unexpectedly and knock the ---- out of the man who's been playing about with your wife. Change his face, Corporal."

'Dear Johns' were often received and pasted on the squadron notice board, a total of twenty such letters within the first six months.

---

[52] The Labour party came to power in 1945. The Conservatives promised to effect almost mass de-mobilization within a short space of time. Obviously people would flood the employment market and be offered derisory wages. Many recalled the 30s when gaffers could pose the question "What will you work for, chap?". Non-union 'shops' would flourish operated by unscrupulous employers. The Labour party promised to de-mob. using numbers: first in – first out! In any event the 'present emergency' did not end for many years.

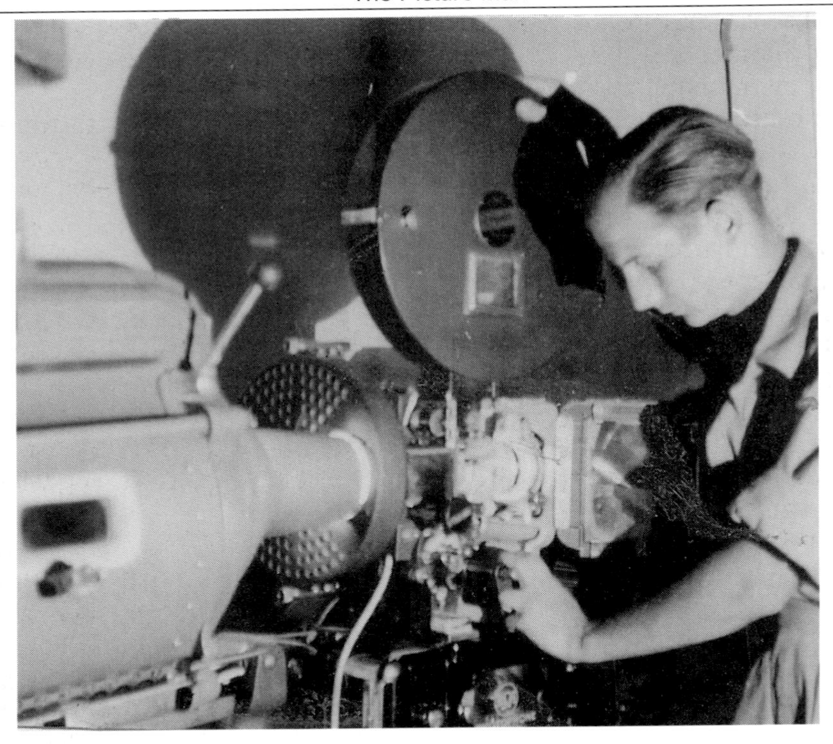

The author threading the rear-shutter machine in the outdoor cinema box

Many uneducated women back home thought that their husbands and sweethearts could be romancing glamorous Arab girls. Separations of a few months played havoc with relationships regarding trust and was only part of the equation. Loneliness over years produced an insoluble simultaneous equation. Life consisted of a treadmill: billet—cookhouse—work—cookhouse—billet!

Apart from the squadron, 'Habb.' housed many hangers, servicing wings, transport command, and the R.A.F. Levies Armoured car division. The Group Captain commanding insisted the cinema opened nightly without fail, essential for morale. This being the case one failed to understand the incompetence of the 'mandarins' in Whitehall. The heat warped the wooden fuselages of the Mosquitos, which were scrapped. Before amazed Iraqis we smashed the Rolls Royce Merlin engines with sledgehammers. A total waste of money, since they fitted Lancasters which had been modified as the 'York' passenger and mail transport. 249 squadron was without aircraft for over four months, as the Mosquitoes were replaced by single seater rocket-firing Tempests which the aircrew could not fly, and after months of delay the Mosquito spare parts arrived!

The same incompetents did not post any projectionists to run the show – civilian or otherwise. They dispatched new equipment for the box including a monstrosity of an arc lamp – the 'Lumm'! Third-rate junk. So hot we needed asbestos gloves to adjust or renew the carbons almost twenty minutes after switch-off. Supposedly automatic, they required more attention than a hand-fed arc.

Changing over all the equipment from the outdoor box to indoors was a straight-forward chore. At the end of the second hot season (mid-September 1947) dust storms intensified and the screen was ripped to ribbons during the final double reel. I carried on projecting while the entire audience left coughing and choking with fine dust. We moved the equipment indoors having no choice with continuing winds. Very warm for patrons indoors!

On opening the tabs I experienced an unforgettable shock. Universal's trade-mark appeared a wishy-washy mess. I glanced swiftly at the arc: the douser[53] was up and the shutter fully open. Within seconds I closed the tabs and shut down. The screen had been stolen! First house abandoned. For two hours Iraqi refreshment attendants, myself, and Ft. Sgt. Povey, the manager, plastered the brick wall in matt white paint. A packed second house was difficult due to the arcs: the heat from them meant we could only carbon up at the last minute before change-over, and several were missed for that reason. Lumm arcs – ughh!

The following night I projected onto the painted brickwork, but next day a replacement screen arrived from Cairo. I penned a weekly bulletin for the squadron notice-board listing the film programmes with a thumbnail story synopsis. This particular week I added—"Kindly inform Yours Truly, or the Military Police, if you see any Iraqis wearing perforated canvas suits."

The cinema committee met in the first week of each month (I represented the squadron almost from my arrival at 'Habb'). Early October I asked the officer-in-charge for permission to visit Salman's boss in Baghdad with a view to keeping the Strong 'Utility' arcs by cash payment or on lease—if possible all the projection equipment. He agreed, gave me *carte blanche* to arrange a deal of some kind,

---

[53] Douser - a steel plate which covered the arc-lamp mirror, protecting it from cracking by spitting particles of hot copper –especially when burning-in the carbons.

and I travelled on the dusty bumpy road to the city surrounded by service newcomers fresh from the U.K.

"So what's the place like?" asked one of the 'erks[54] concerning Baghdad. "Any bints?" queried another. These boys needed months to 'get their knees brown'. I couldn't resist playing a cruel hoax. "Ah! Bints! Arabic for girls... you're learning fast. Girls everywhere. You'll see fat Greek women pass by in the rear of taxis – Arabs adore big ladies. Oh, the girls! Slim gorgeous girls! Plenty of 'talent'," I lied.

Everywhere one walked in the infamous city the streets were thronged with men wearing long grubby shirts and the fez. I doubted any one of them would pay a return visit. Not a female anywhere.

"Like Yvonne de Carlo?" one asked eagerly. "Do they wear flimsy pantaloons. You know, in the night-clubs."

"Do they! Just you wait," I promised with a dead-pan face, being more concerned with my mission to retain the equipment.

The cinema, a converted theatre, had two circles; beneath them twenty twirling fans with large fins: ten more in the ceiling. In the box Salman operated twin Simplex Super E7s at a steep rake throw to an elongated screen well masked to counteract the slight distortion. On an out-size spool without a fireproof box was four thousand feet of nitrate slowly clicking through the gate as he lit a match nonchalantly, to smoke a black cheroot. A boy, barely twelve years of age, was rewinding a huge reel, and another, ten years at most, sat beside a slide lantern showing Arabic sub-titles. He moved these each time a loud splice passed through the gate. Salman explained that these joints were a whole frame overlap, thus creating a loud snap for the child to take as a signal to change the dialogue slide. They were showing *all 13 chapters* in 260 minutes of *Junior G-men of the Air*.[55]

I followed Salman to the office, passing through the auditorium where an audience of some eighty Arabs chatted loudly in an effort to hear themselves competing with the over-loud sound. Everyone appeared to be smoking – pipes, cigars and cigarettes; the obnoxious mixture of smoke and sweaty bodies amid the stifling heat defies description.

Iraqi men saved money for many years in order to buy a wife. For many, it was over thirty years before this became possible.

---

[54] slang for an airman who had recently joined the service. First year – erk. A. C. Two

[55] Universal 1942: Ray Taylor

Homosexuality was rife, and brothels in the city quite an industry. I asked Salman about the muslim religious attitude regarding virgin brides retaining blood-stained bed sheets after the wedding night. Was it true if the bride was not a virgin her groom may demand a refund and the girl be sold to a brothel? "Oh yes! It happens" he said, and gave me a wink. "Wife and I used pig's blood."

After reading the Koran much of it seemed logical to a degree, yet a religion condemning alcohol and punishing women was difficult for a westerner to contemplate or understand.

Salman left me in the stuffy office of the owner whose arabic name I cannot recall: a well-dressed, fat man barely five feet in height, red-faced, balding and in his mid-fifties. He spoke excellent English and greeted me as though a brother. "I am delighted to meet you, effendi. Salman, he say, about equipment. We make a good deal, eh? A reasonable fee, eh?"

Subject to my officer's approval 100 dinars monthly was agreed. He poured me a glass of Arak (a powerful Arabic white wine) to toast the agreement. One mouthful was sufficient. Arak – ugh! Kick like a mule! We shook hands.

"You will be my guest, of course. Let me arrange overnight accommodation for you at our best hotel – and for your utmost pleasure a girl and boy, not yet thirteen, both clean and Christians. You use as you wish – very nice, eh?"

* * * * *

As a certain Sunday newspaper used to write: I made my excuses and left.

* * * * * * *

7: Get Some In!

A pair of chameleons made their home in the box of the outdoor show. These reptiles fascinated me. The male possessed a large and small horn above the mouth, and unlike me they could look in all directions at once. At least I rarely saw a fly. I was aware of technical difficulties in the squadron while making up programmes in the rewinding room downstairs (exactly as at the Regal), as a Super Simplex E7 delivered the make-believe upon the screen. Thus I was like a chameleon in effect, leading a double life.

Aircraft rely wholly on electrics, from landing lights, flaps, guns, instruments, etc. plus some 15 miles of electric wiring. Carrying out a daily inspection on an aircraft is all-important: each trade expert signs for serviceability for engines, instruments, rigging, W. T. and electrics. Counter-signed by the Flight Sergeant, the chit is accepted and signed for in turn by the pilot. Should any disaster occur due to the negligence of the ground crew a court martial was certain. I adopted a similar D. I. for the cinema: who rewound each spool, checked each splice, and which member of my crew projected. My forms, carbon-copied in the Orderly Room, were religiously kept exactly the same as box procedure for ABC.

In 1947 my team consisted of a Corporal and two Sergeants (out-ranking me, a mere L.A.C.–equivalent army rank being Lance-Corporal). Rank didn't matter: we referred to each other as Tom, Dick or Harry. I couldn't use the title of Chief, as 'Chief' or 'Chiefy' in R.A.F. jargon means Flight Sergeant, so I was First Operator: in fact we used our positions and names exactly as Americans. 'First Op. Northover', 'Second Op. White', and so forth.

The complement was six: three operators each evening. I projected Saturdays, both houses, alone. Monday to Wednesday I was in the box (and seated in the show every night if not on duty for squadron night flying) and watched both houses, always noting discrepancies in projection, such as a badly-lit screen or unobserved 'racks'. A bad rack (the dividing line between each frame could be observed on screen; the picture not fitting the black masking completely) annoyed me, and if it was not corrected after a minute I would leave my seat and tongue-lash the man on the machine. They were paid an extra £2 per week—I made sure they earned it! After training they knew a missed changeover meant dismissal, like a lightning court martial. Recruits for box work were plentiful, not only for extra pay, but to reduce the monotony at Habb., devoid of female company.

First Op. Northover, F/Sgt Povey (manager) and 'gash type'

Audience reaction is all-important. Many projectionists are unaware of this factor, but I found this a most interesting facet of the cinema. From the box one knew how bored the audience were by the flare of matches and lighters as they lit tobacco. This was very noticeable in a Bogart film, and not due to impatience regarding pace produced by the director. Each time 'Bogey' lit a cigarette one noticed a score or more of patrons lighting-up. A hush developed during moments of characters creeping around using a torch in the dark of mystery thrillers, accompanied sometimes by a special musical score. I was amazed how often a belly-laugh obliterated the continuing dialogue, usually more hilarious than the first laughter line. Audiences unwittingly cheated themselves of more laughter. Obviously I was never more aware of their reaction than this show at 'Habb'.

Cat-calls were numerous from an all-male audience—especially in love scenes. Gary Cooper always portrayed a slow character, and his romantic sequences were almost slow motion. “Go on! Kiss her, mate.” “Wish I had the chance. Go on!” When the first clinch happened the roar of approval could be heard out-of-doors for half a mile, somewhat like a football crowd. This annoyed many folk who were unable to hear the ensuing dialogue. Whenever a romance was booked friends would ask me, “This film tonight, *Laura*.[56] Is it a love story?” Assured the Vera Caspary novel had been superbly brought to life as a first-class thriller they attended.

The cinema committee meetings were fraught with many unanswerable questions. Who books the films? Why no double features? Why must we suffer serials only fit for juveniles? Why do we never see a newsreel – if it's a month old who cares? Newsreels please!

Although immersed in projection work, I have always preferred the stage to these shadows in the dark. Visiting the Northampton Repertory Theatre[57] I was introduced to the live stage from the age of six. My collection of programmes has been kept for many decades. Like so many reps, this theatre helped many later featured players and stars to learn their craft. Several household names emerged from here, Errol Flynn, Freda Jackson, and David Tomlinson among them.

Here at Habb. I learned ciné-variety for the first time—the hard way. Organ interludes were easy, stage lighting for musical shows and plays quite a different proposition. Stage presentations were given indoors, monthly from October to March. The screen was not removed, for a black backcloth was easily lowered across it and the speakers placed in the wings. Four rows of battens were available, plus the inevitable footlights.

The first show proved easy, as no lighting plot was necessary for ‘Professor’ Schaffer, hypnotist, who wanted full stage lighting. His act was the old chestnut of lining up twenty patrons and having each perform various actions – polishing buttons, hammering nails in wood, and so on. This piece consumed an hour. After an interval, variations on a theme – mind-reading the audience at random. Two performances, and both were full houses. Schaffer received publicity

---

[56] T.C.F. 1944: Otto Preminger. Clifton Webb becoming a star late in life, acting everyone off the screen with this compelling characterization as Waldo Hydecker, the columnist with a pen dipped in acid.

[57] Established in the old Opera House in 1927, subsidized by the Town and Corporation. In the late 70s fortnightly rep. became a season of 7 or 8 productions, with a very successful 6 week panto run in addition.

through articles in the *Air Force News*. Apparently, he was a German psychiatrist, and readers' letters argued he ought to be gainfully employed medically.

The next show—a straight play *While Parents Sleep*—was no challenge for an artistic lighting apprentice. Only two limes, poorly lit, fixed on either side of the circle were worse than useless. I planned to improve these before the following winter. E.N.S.A. touring companies visited frequently and the lack of a strongly-lit lime was most conspicuous by its absence, plus a skilled operator.

Throughout 1947 and into 1948 the R.A.F. Cinema Corporation sprang to life with recent film releases and occasionally threw in ancient copies of *Pathé News,* in particular a reel featuring the prolonged seven weeks of deep snow the U.K. suffered in that infamous winter. Whatever the length of the feature, serials were shown; always Columbia or Universal and churned out by directors Ford Beebe or Ray Taylor.

Feisal, the twelve year-old boy King of Iraq,[58] visited the squadron with his uncle, the Prince Regent. The air force completely rebuilt an ancient Anson, including a mainplane change. Although having played no part in the reconstruction, I wangled a place on the air test. Alighting, accidentally I caught my 'chute's rip cord ring. A £2 fine from safety equipment workers, dragged along in the wind and dust. The 'chute had to be re-packed.

Most of my associates in the squadron were being demobbed apart from myself and instrument tradesmen. Another slip-up at the Air Ministry created a shortage of electricians and some other trades were held back from release for up to a year. General Duty men, same demob group as mine, were in civvy street eighteen months before me. I was never home-sick, and detest the climate of the U.K. I became impatient, however, wondering how many villages might be left available for a travelling cinema.

Before the hot season in early September my ordered routine was suddenly shattered. Everything went haywire within one week. There were technical faults on two Tempests. One crashed during night flying: luckily no fatalities. Fortunately, the landing lamps worked well allowing the other kites to see the flare path over the glare of burning wreckage. I had a sleepless night.

The following evening, a Friday, was extremely hot with dust storms. Too early for transferring equipment at the show indoors. I

[58] Assassinated in 1958.

was packing up the programme at 11 o'clock when a civilian entered the rewinding room, an engineer by the name of Morgan. He was surprised to know I knew nothing of his visit to change over the equipment—arcs, heads, sound system and speakers—next day commencing at eleven p.m. and working all night in readiness for Sunday opening. Films required make-up for both houses Saturday, and when I returned to the billet I suffered an entire night without sleep. Airmen newly posted to the squadron played cards amid much shouting until 3.30 a.m., so I was barely asleep before work started on aircraft: two with electrical faults.

I always operated alone for the two Saturday houses (same programme), thus resting my team. Many watched the show or enjoyed a free time at the lake in a Malcomm (rest) club, whatever. After suffering several sleepless nights I felt groggy and found difficulty in concentrating. Losing sleep in the tropics can present serious problems. Twice I almost missed a changeover. Morgan was underfoot with brochures regarding the new equipment which had arrived, filling the rewind room and box—a new pair of Lumm arc lamps and Kalee 11 Indomitable heads. The Simplex heads were the only prize secured from my Baghdad excursion.

After making-up films Salman arrived and invited me to tea. I almost fell asleep, dropping a plate of cakes on the floor. His wife, who could not speak English, was tearful about moving to the city and losing her home. They had a boy of twelve and a girl of thirteen. The Salmans lived well compared to other Iraqis, as his cinema wages tripled those of his associates chiefly engaged in manual trades.

"She no want Baghdad, Mister Arthur. Scared for children. We can't stay here any more. We apart for meals at city cinema, she and children here. No good! You look ill, Mister Arthur."

As the final reel was ending, I thought *four* chameleons were clinging to the box walls. The picture appeared out of focus. Several times, leaning against the wall beside a viewing port soaked in perspiration I began to lose concentration—about to go to sleep standing, like a horse.

Morgan startled me. I jumped in a dazed fashion "You all right?" he said. I nodded and decided to go for a swim to refresh myself and shake off this drowsy attitude. For some time I floated around on my back in the dimly-lit, deserted pool. The moon was up affording a ghostly light. All was strangely quiet compared to the usual shouts of men playing water polo and diving around. When dressed I began to perspire freely. the thought of returning home did not appeal: back to freezing wet cold Blighty. The service had a phrase for bods such as me—'sand happy'. After a few months leave to return to the cinema and squadron would be ideal. So much to do arranging stage lighting, and I had written some revue sketches which I hoped a travelling company may use if considered suitable.

Throughout the night Morgan and myself laboured continually, finally viewing the break of dawn smoking cigarettes. Cats were copulating in the shrubbery.

"They've the right idea," he observed. "Are you due for a spot of leave?"

"No, not yet. I've not taken a leave since I arrived here. Just a three day 'hitch-hike' to Karachi." [59]

"Haven't been to India."

"Don't bother. Those people back home planning to tour the world if they win a fortune on the pools ugh! India would break their hearts. Children sewing garments, and hammering metal for jewel boxes for twelve to fourteen hours daily. As for the poverty! It's disgraceful. Tried to find an old friend without success!"

I walked back to the billet hatless. We wore large-brimmed 'bush head gear' at all times. The temperature exceeded 115° shade. Seventy-two hours without sleep sapped my strength, especially after the exertions helping to effect the changeover. Tempest K105 had an electrical snag. I had grounded this the previous day, so I decided to sort it out and sleep all afternoon. The evening's films had been made-up as I spooled off Saturday's feature.

At six a.m. a corporal met me as I was leaving the cookhouse after breakfast, about to enter a hangar. "Here you are, mate. Home you go, lucky man!" He handed me a clearance chit.

"Go home? Talk sense. I'm up to my neck in work!"

"You're on demob. Finished! Need to report to transport command by five o'clock. Dakota leaves for Cairo tomorrow. Here you are. Get cracking!"

I stared in disbelief at the long list of sections, twelve in all, which were required to sign the chit. In the army one was checked out from the guard room. Not so in the air force.

I had not cleared a station since Nairobi, where each section, medical centre, library stores, etc. were in a compact unit. At Habb. it

[59] One could fly on service aircraft with written permission understanding that no life insurance was covered, only for air crew. I also enjoyed a '48hr.' without permission to Johannesburg on a French kite to and from Nairobi with 'Taffy' Coles.

was a mile walk to stores, another half-mile to the education office, and so on. On a Sunday? I knew how many signatures might be difficult to obtain.

I decided to clear and see the C.O., Squadron Leader Fitzpatrick, an excellent type, and try to stay for at least another week. Had I done so, no doubt the nightmare which followed might have been averted. I wandered the large camp, chit in hand and hatless. At the medical centre I jabbered incoherently about arc lamps and an aircraft with an 'electrical short'. A corporal, one of my cinema team, was typing rapidly and ignored me.

"Can't go home. New projectors. Been swimming. Lousy breakfast. Need this chit signed. Seeing the C.O. Two kites grounded. Trouble everywhere," I said.

A doctor rolled up my sleeve and gave me an injection. I vaguely recall waking up in the hospital abed. An elderly nurse reminded me of my mother. "Hullo, Mam." I said. "Why am I home? I've much work to complete."

Flt. Sergeant Povey and another member of my team stood beside my bed. "Who are you? Oh, Povey! Should be managing the cinema," I said excitedly.

"Give me your arm, airman," ordered the nurse. Her eyes stared into mine. She reminded me of Cicely Oates, the actress who appeared with Peter Lorre in the original version of *The Man Who Knew Too Much*.[60] Another injection and oblivion once more.

I remember being taken in a wheelchair to a Dakota. A dozen friends clustered about me. Cries of "You'll soon be O.K. in Blighty." "Cheer up, you're going home." Someone mentioned heatstroke.

* * * * *

The flight was bumpy and at some 30,000' bitterly cold. There are misty recollections of a meal in Palestine with two medical orderlies who sat on either side. Awakening hours later, I found myself in bed once more. I asked an army corporal nurse concerning my whereabouts and the day of the week.

"You're in the nuthouse, Brylcreem boy. Up the pole. Trying to work your ticket. Met your kind before."[61]

---

[60] G-B. 1934: Alfred Hitchcock for Gaumont

[61] Pretending illness to return home and be invalided out of the service.

He made me drink a tiny glass of liquid. I did so and collapsed into sleep within a few minutes. Awakening during the night, bursting to urinate, I staggered about falling on the bed of another patient. In the dim blue light I observed twenty beds, ten each side of the ward. The corporal approached me. I asked to use the toilet.

"Let me help you piss, airman!" He punched me in the stomach. I doubled up in pain and urinated. "You filthy pig" he growled. After being stripped, and wearing a long white gown, I was thrown back upon the bed and fell asleep.

Next morning several army medics stood about my bed. I asked to see an intelligent N.C.O. or officer. "An intelligence officer!" exclaimed one of them. "He thinks he's a spy! His breath stinks. Give him a drink." Another injection and everything became a black whirlpool.

Some hours later I learned from a German psychiatrist this was a closed mental ward. The ten beds opposite contained Germans. The consultant spoke good English and I helped an orderly supply tea and biscuits to his patients. One poor devil leaped from his bed, stood upright, arms over his head, screaming. "Rescued from a submarine. Thinks it's water," I was told.

My complaint about the behaviour of the corporal fell upon deaf ears. "He's on leave for a week," said a tall, thin German orderly. "A very nasty man, Corporal Palmer." I promised myself I would catch up with this sadistic swine somehow somewhere someday for revenge.

The hospital ship *Devonshire* ploughed its way past stormy Biscay. A demented army man somehow escaped from the closed ward and leapt into the raging sea – never to be rescued. After docking we patients were transferred to London by hospital train. A Red Cross nurse supplied me with cigarettes in the Egyptian Army Hospital. By helping the German doctor he arranged my transfer to the open ward. The closed wards there, aboard ship, and on the train, were grim.

Anyone committed to such institutions could not be easily freed. No one wished to listen one to another. Harsh treatment constantly repeated, and no method to address one's grievances. *A disgrace to the medical profession at that time.*

My mother and sister visited me at another such hospital at Banstead. They received notification from the war office informing them I was dangerously ill. I found this incredible. All I required was sleep. The whole experience was similar to the Academy Award-winning *The Snake Pit.* [62]

[62] TCF 1948: Anatole Litvak

A high-ranking medical officer at Gloucester explained that I was wrongly diagnosed at 'Habb'. "It was heatstroke, airman ... nothing more. Mind you, this report of you staggering around telling people you refused to go home – really! You'll be medically grade 3 for six months. Why not take on a seven-year engagement? The service is so short of electricians. By the way, tradesmen who go to bits on security squadrons are usually examined under psychiatric conditions. If you marry, I suggest you do not have children for three to five years." He signed my release book in the absence of my C.O. – a few words quickly jotted down "Has done some work in camp cinemas."

Over fifty years were to pass before I joined the Habbaniya Society to learn that the cinema eventually installed CinemaScope. Perhaps the place is open and operated by the son of Salman for the Iraqi air force?

The 'Habb.' outdoor box by day – a distinctly dodgy-looking cable lash-up!

8: Demob happy

"The job pays a fiver weekly. You'll be co-chief with Bob Munn. O.K.?" snapped the manager of the Regal, Northampton, two weeks after my demob from the R.A.F. Ten years had passed since I worked in the box here as an eager schoolboy. In the 30s a chief had earned five pounds weekly, and pay had remained stationary. Now owned by the Southan Morris group, they were offering a measly tenner for two skilled technicians to operate seven day showing continuous from 1.30-11p.m. Some deal!

I recalled visiting the town centre Exchange (later the Gaumont) with the chief of the Savoy, who invited his opposite number to join N.A.T.K.E.[63] "Your show is termed an 'A' house, and mine a 'B'. So following union rates you earn a bare fiver and here I'm guaranteed four pounds. Forget it! I work for Gaumont at over six quid. ABC were always a crappy set-up. Unions? Rubbish!"

Pre-war, one wondered why a threatened strike for better pay and conditions was never organised. From this brief conversation one can easily understand the anomalies concerned for a union with no 'clout'—a half-hearted effort in the Midlands planned pre-1939 failed. Unlike our continental counter-parts, particularly the French, we British never stick together except with our backs to the wall as in WWII.

The job would suffice until I completed arrangements for my mobile cinema operation, so it was back to square one as I recommenced projection at the Regal with Bob Munn; a man who was to help me considerably in becoming a successful mobile showman.

Bob is difficult to describe in a few words. Barely 5' 4" in height with receding, thinning hair, blue eyes, possessing an engaging personality, he was an electrical genius. Two years my senior he served as a squadron electrician at home and abroad, and left the air force a year earlier than my own release. Naturally, we had no other staff and within hours worked nicely together, becoming firm friends.

Describing him as a genius may be a sweeping statement, yet anyone who knew him would agree. Unlike no other electrician one may meet in a lifetime, Bob easily worked on complicated circuits without a wiring diagram. Soldering iron in hand he would remove

[63] The National Association of Theatrical and Kinematograph Employees

condensers, boosters, coils, resistances, and rectifiers as someone sorting through a large bag of toffees. Piles of components of all kinds littered the bench in the Regal's box, for he would spend hours in electrical junk shops: gadgets everywhere. The show used all B.T-H. equipment.[64] "I've improved the sound system—a few amendments here and there." I wondered how he dared mess with first- and second-stage amplification, claiming to know more than the designer—yet he did!

Within a month he invited me to tea at his council house in Roade, six miles south of Northampton. I met his wife 'Rene and their five children who seemed to be any- and every-where at once. Three clustered around the outdoor coal shed, where, hidden behind half a ton of anthracite, were fifty 1,000' cans of inflammable nitrate film. "My film dump. All that's left of my cinema which failed."

Poor Bob had invested his R.A.F. gratuity and savings into an old building in Earl's Barton (population 3,000) with a partner. Here they exhibited cheap programmes from Butcher's Film Service of Manchester: ancient war-time comedies starring Frank Randle and others of these music hall 'heroes of comedy' on flat-rate prices. These attracted only a minority, since villagers were able to visit Wellingborough's four cinemas only three miles distant. The place became a motor garage and showroom carrying on a successful business to the present day.

Bob handed me some cans of film. "Reels One to Five, Arth. I'll bring in the other four. Come into the 'box'. I followed him into the kitchen. Here a Kalee 7 projector with arc

Two views of the building that was once Bob Munn's Earl's Barton Cinema
Photographed in Summer 2001 by Llewellyn Williams

[64] British Thomson-Houston Ltd. of Rugby

lamp and two speakers filled the room. "What do you think of it? See the arc? No carbons, no need, I've made up a special lamp. One day cinemas will dispense with carbon arcs, you'll see!"

" 'Rene," he called to his wife, who was wrapping a nappy around the latest addition to the family, lying quietly as a doll across her lap. "I'm going to run your favourite star tonight—Gracie Fields in *Look Up and Laugh.*[65]

"Lovely! Haven't seen it for months," she replied. Bob asked me to follow him upstairs. Two small rooms with beds were surrounded by cans of film. "I've ten features: 'won' all of them from here and there."

We returned downstairs and out to the garden shed, to view a veritable museum of cinema memorabilia; several large wax discs from the early days of sound, arc lamps, three projector heads, dozens of old posters, and hundreds of stills from productions of the 30s.

"How about this, Arth.? A magic lantern sheet and a pile of slides. The kids love watching these. The sheet is yours on loan."

A puzzling gift. He read my thoughts. "For the mobile. How can you transport a screen using a motor-cycle combination? You should buy a car or best of all a van."

I explained in much detail how a motor-cycle combination could drive through bad weather: thick fog, icy roads, in fact snowy conditions, and he knew that my finances were insufficient to buy or run a van. In Scotland, during my R.A.F. service, combinations tackled very bad weather.

After a few months at the Regal I planned carefully my first show date. Being reasonably good at art some twenty posters were painted in the box in between change-overs. "Water-colour will run in the rain—use printing ink and break it down with pure turps," Bob advised. Roughly A6, the posters were completed for *The Spy in White.*[66] Bob made other useful suggestions. "James Mason's all the rage—paint his name in huge letters, and use small print for the title. Don't give the certificate, I read in *Kine Weekly* that censorship doesn't affect 16mm. Did you see this ad. for a special 2½hr. non-stop reel with stand powered by a separate 90v. motor? It'd be perfect—no stops to thread up the next reel. Terrific invention. Look! Only £48!

Borrowing almost £200 from Mother I purchased a B.T-H. 301 machine with 500 watt lamp, ordered through Filmhire Ltd., who sold projectors to the town and county schools. (The two men who ran this

---

[65] Associated Talking Pictures 1935: Basil Dean
[66] a.k.a Search of Stamboul 1936 Andrew Marton

Jeyes' the Chemist's subsidiary were Mr. Jacklin and Mr. Smith. The latter had retired from many years as second operator at the Gaumont—my favourite childhood cinema.) The company purchased a large library of 16mm. shorts and fifty feature films—the most recent of these being eleven years old.

It was Mr. Jacklin who delivered the exceptionally heavy 301 to me at the Regal. Together with a moving-coil loudspeaker and large transformer the total weight exceeded 2 cwt. The day it arrived I operated the matinée alone in the box while Bob made up a Saturday children's matinée in the rewind room below. Ever inventive, his pulleys and cable lifted up and returned each spool somewhat like the style of a dumb waiter. At four o'clock I went downstairs as he was spending a lot of time apparently putting twelve reels together.

"Have you a bad copy? Oh, no! What have you done?" I cried. I stood motionless shocked beyond description: the B.T-H. was in pieces. Valves were strewn around the bench, tiny condensers everywhere, and the lamphouse was a few pieces of buckled metal.

"Don't worry, Arth. It's no good. I'm making a few amendments." After shouting in temper, suddenly I sat down on the bottom concrete step as he brushed past. "Don't forget the show, Arth.! Touch nothing."

I tried not to go to pieces like the brand-new projector. It was difficult not to cry: the six inch circumference sound drum turned freely without its large sprocket which lay on the floor. Leaving the room and slamming the door behind me I wandered down the circle steps into the street and lit a cigarette. A few patrons were buying tickets while others outside studied the stills for *Road to Rio.*[67] After walking into the town in a dazed state I came to the conclusion that Bob could restore the projector to its original condition. Returning to the clicking celluloid in the box I found Bob laughing. "When we finish tonight you'll be thrilled with my modifications, you'll see!"

"Bob, its brand-new—was brand-new."

"Arth., take the show and we'll try out your B.T-H. I've a South African newsreel on 16mm. to use. More sound as well, this thing won't give 10 watts, but I've an old amp. to match up. Look again at the G-B. film hire catalogue you've got. Many entries are 'poor sound, fit only for small rooms.' As for the lamphouse, it needs a 750 watt. We can throw the sound-drum sprocket away. Quite unnecessary! A

---

[67] Paramount 1947: Norman McCloud

bad copy with several joints'll jam on it or jump off. Just leave everything to me!"

I had no choice. The programme churned through the heads as though in slow motion. Only once did I leave the box to see how he was progressing: with a soldering-iron in one hand and a thin screwdriver between his teeth he grinned nodding his head for me to return upstairs.

The feature finished at 10.45, and fifteen minutes later I watched an old newsreel in the rewinding room. Crisp, even sound, and a steady well-lit picture reproduced on the rear of an old quad poster he'd affixed to the wall.[68]

"Notice the spring-loaded claw. If on a bad copy you lose a loop before or after the film runs through the gate just pull the film like this." With a finger he pulled the moving film adjusting the loops from the main claw. "See how easy it is? Doesn't damage the film sprockets. The claw disengages. Best idea the B.T-H. people have had. We must find out if 750 or 1000 watt lamps are available."

I returned home much relieved. A few days later I visited Guildford by rail to purchase the non-stop equipment. How I managed to change stations in London carrying it I cannot imagine in retrospect. More awkward than heavy, the items consisted of an electric motor attached to a bracket to fit beneath a heavy steel stand with four telescopic legs. This I carried in one hand together with the motor, using the other hand to lift the three-foot-square tin box containing two spools, each capable of holding four 1600 ft. reels.

In the mid-40s my mother had re-married, and my step-father and I were like father and son. I referred to him as 'Dad'. A skilled motor engineer, he was in charge of maintenance for the police vehicles at Northampton Borough. I mention him and Bob because without their joint expertise my mobile cinema would have never become a worthwhile operation.

Only a week after the Guildford journey Dad visited Nottingham to purchase a BSA 500cc. motor-cycle. It was an ex-army machine finished in camouflage colours and had never been used, costing a mere £50 compared to a new model at £200! Also, he fitted a discarded G.P.O. box side-car bought for another £50. The cinema equipment fitted inside perfectly.

Meanwhile, back in the 'box' during projection, Bob helped me with various ideas and hints. The posters, long since prepared, were now

[68] Posters are now collectable items – e.g. Casablanca auctioned at Sotheby's for £4,000, Chaplin's The Gold Rush for £40,000

covered in small messages which Bob scrawled on them using a felt-tip pen: *Perfect sound! Non-stop performance! Regular shows to be arranged! Your own Village Cinema! Save bus-fare money! Midgetone Mobile Movies!*

He frowned and gave me a puzzled glance. "Why Midgetone, Arth.?" I explained the name originated from a magazine article I read whilst abroad headed *The March of the Midget Movies*, describing the thousands of mobile film shows taking to the road.

Deciding to arrange a try-out performance venue proved easy; so many sizeable villages were available eight miles from town I was spoiled for choice. I settled for Brixworth, booked the village hall for a Wednesday night at fifty shillings, and distributed posters with free tickets to each shop and pub throughout the place. I fixed three posters on tree trunks at excellent locations. The feature film and shorts cost £3 for a single performance, cheaper on a sliding scale for several shows. Visiting Customs & Excise I purchased pads of tickets at a cost of £5, as there was 11d. entertainment tax on a ticket that sold for 1/9d!

* * * * *

While Bob carried on as usual for my day off, I arrived at the hall with my equipment. Due to commence at 7.30, 4 p.m. gave me sufficient time to ensure everything was in place without any mis-haps. I staggered the hundred chairs so patrons would enjoy a clear view of the screen, while the 16' square lantern sheet proved ideal hung with sixteen cords - four a side – fastened to an iron girder at the top and a wooden form at the bottom. Within minutes of hanging, many creases had disappeared. At 5 p.m. the supporting travelogue appeared most professional, the only discrepancy being the weak light from the 500w. lamp, particularly noticeable when running the first reel of the feature.

Bob's mains-dropper resistance feeding 90v. to the large-spool motor was fixed to a separate amplifier from his collection; matched with the projector this gave up to 20 watts of sound if required.[69] Projecting half-an-hour of the feature proved the point. Alternate reels from the 35mm. original varied considerably: part one quite good, part two indistinct with muffled voices, and part three as reel one. I was

[69] The B.T-H. 301 output was 10 watts, and under-powered for poorly-printed sound-tracks.

thankful for Bob's extra amplifier despite the inevitable roar of sound in scenes void of dialogue and background music.

Suddenly I heard the telephone and answered its strident bell immediately. A lady with a plummy voice asked "Can you tell me what time the Mason film is screened?" I gave the time mentioning the supporting programme and prices as she interrupted quickly, "Eight ten. Thank you so much."

Were the carriage trade going to arrive? Might be a sell-out. More chairs were available in a kitchen and a small room, and with two long wooden forms placed against the wall the place provided 120 seats. Parking was available for at least ten cars.

As advertised, the doors opened at 7.15 for a 7.30 start. Outside a few pieces of paper rubbish blew about in an icy wind, and no other movement whatsoever. A few drops of rain in the wind induced a certain foreboding. Wet nights always reduced trade. A tall man approached. Almost 7.20 and one patron—surely not. He was the caretaker.

"I've come to light the radiators," he said abruptly, carried out this chore and left saying, "Bring the keys up to my house when you've finished, mate. These heaters'll turn off after an hour." As he left two lady pensioners entered. By 7.30 twelve adults and twenty children had arrived. Several children when buying tickets asked, "Do the pictures talk?" Having no space to carry a record-player, the hall echoed with over-loud voices.

"I washed me feet before I came out," shouted an obvious lady pensioner to her friend, amid chattering children who fidgeted about on the chairs. Rows of empty seats, a screen without tabs: how crude the place appeared. Time to start. I checked the thread-up. All was well except for the pitiful attendance. About to switch off the light a queue of some twenty teenagers purchased tickets.

When they were seated I opened up the projector and raced to the light switches as the children gave a loud cheer. Before the 'full supporting programme' finished another dozen adults, some with children, arrived. The exchange of coins and mumbling of patrons, together with chairs noisily moved about was irritating and distracting for those watching the travelogue.

Things settled down somewhat when the feature started. After a few minutes, when Mason appeared a woman exclaimed in a loud voice, "Doesn't he look young?" "It's such an old film. He was a teenager." Among other remarks including "I've seen this donkey's years ago" and occasional requests "Be quiet! We want to hear the film, not you," the large spool turned rapidly as the final two reels raced through. Twice I left the machine, torch in hand, to try and stop the children running in and out of the lavatories beside the screen. They would leave the door open and a shaft of light fell across the screen.

A small girl sat crying, "It's my brother," she sobbed, "He's wet his trousers." Before I could handle this situation I heard a clattering from the 301 as the picture slithered about on the screen. A thick splice had caused loss of loop. I hurried to the stand and pulled the film regaining the loop thankful the B.T-H. was so well designed with the retractable claw.

Hours later after unloading and carrying the equipment upstairs to my bedroom I wound off the films, carefully replacing leaders and trailers placing them ready for parcel post. I counted the takings. Allowing for film and hall hire the profit amounted to a few shillings! No allowance for petrol, travelling, or wear and tear: the total profit was nil. As I fell asleep late that night I pondered about the voice over the telephone. Surely if the lady attended she would never do so again! After the hours of preparation plus the expense involved, I knew this performance would be my first and last mobile picture show.

Lois sitting (pensively?) in the side-car outside Arthur's mother's house in Wycliffe Road, Northampton. Wellingborough Road is in the background. (The author claims Lois *loved* travelling in this manner. When this is said, out of his eye-line, her eyes roll heaven-wards!)

* * * * * * *

9: The March of *Midgetone Mobile Movies*

Many weeks passed by working the Regal with Bob. I decided to rejoin the air force if possible, and compiled a lengthy classified for the advertisement section of *Mini Cinema,* a free pamphlet for 16mm. film exhibitors in *Kinematograph Weekly:*

> *B.T-H. 301 16mm. sound projector with additional amplifier and long-play attachment capable of showing over two hours continuous film. Cost: £270. Used once only. Owner emigrating. Bargain at £190 or near offer. Box...*

"You ought to ask for £200, Arth." Bob told me between reels. "Anyway, you should think twice about the mob. Don't forget it's peacetime now—marching around the square for daily colour-hoisting. A friend's son is doing his national service; says it's all bullshit. Terrible! You'll not like it." The chance of re-joining 249, an overseas squadron which never returned home, was as hopeless as winning the football pools for three consecutive weeks.

Bob suggested various villages for future try-outs. "No use condemning the mobile over one performance. I think the hall fee excessive at fifty shillings. You've spent ages writing and re-writing this advert. Give things another chance. Operate four villages for try-outs and see what happens. Try again. Book a cheap programme from Filmhire—their catalogue contains reasonable features—offer them £6 for a two-hour show over four days. Surely you can earn more than the fiver Southan Morris pay?."

I told him Customs would make more profit than I, but would consider his proposal. Crumpling up the advertisement, I began to plan appropriate locations. Bob ran the matinées for a fortnight as I toured the county for suitable sites, covering over 200 miles. Many thickly populated villages possessed no hall, while tiny hamlets enjoyed superb entertainment centres. Finally, I decided on the five most likely areas.

Arriving at the cinema one morning, Bob greeted me frantically waving a copy of *Kinematograph Weekly* at me. You're on your way, Arth.! They've scrapped Entertainment Tax!" Apparently Sir Stafford Cripps had abolished the iniquitous impost on villages where the population did not exceed 640 in number to the square acre.

"Bet you're glad you voted Labour eh? How's that from the Chancellor of the Exchequer?" cried Bob excitedly.

Thousands of mobile men and film renters were agog with this welcome, unbelievable news. I left the Regal box never to return. My life changed completely. My cousin, a ladies' hairdresser employed at a town centre shop, introduced me to a gorgeous teenage girl who worked at another branch of the firm. I asked her for a date, without success.

Bob Munn *(centre)* **in characteristic pose: relaxing with a pint of beer and two friends outside a village pub.**

In early 1949 I visited London, after writing to Columbia Pictures, and met Sydney Lomberg, the sales manager. After an hour we agreed an excellent deal. Using their product for a year on a firm block-booking basis, programmes were available at £6 weekly, with my choice of films up to an overall running time of two-and-a-half hours maximum. On his advice I booked serials. Since my childhood Saturday matinées I could not shake off these cliff-hanging soap operas including those shown in Iraq.

Spending an hour in Wardour Street proved interesting before the mid-morning appointment with Columbia. Most of the showrooms have disappeared nowadays, but then, viewing the latest *Kalee* model, the new *Streemlite* arc-lamp, and studying superbly arranged publicity for the last film releases was fascinating.

"So we have a deal," exclaimed Lomberg, "Come along, I'll treat you to lunch." As we walked down 'the Street' and into Old Compton Street we were constantly accosted by prostitutes.

* * * * *

The first mobile round consisted of the following: -

Mondays	Harpole Band Institute	rent	1-0-0	seats 80
Tuesdays	Silverstone Church Hall	rent	15-0	seats 80
Wednesdays	Creaton Village Hall	rent	12-6	seats 100
Thursdays	Hanslope Church Hall	rent	15-0	seats 120
Fridays	Roade British Legion Nissen hut	rent	10-0	seats 70
			£3-12-6	

With films priced at £6-3-6d. (including return postage), and petrol at £2-2-0d (2/6d per gallon), my total weekly expenditure amounted to less than £13. An additional £2 weekly was set aside for projector and exciter lamps, including 2s. for transport spares. The first week's takings, approximately £40, produced a profit of £27. Since the average wage was £8-£9 weekly, this was to become a most lucrative concern.

As sailors are renowned for a girl in every port, I quickly became involved with four different girls from as many locations. One buxom beauty insisted on paying for her ticket plus giving me a gift of a dozen fresh eggs—a young lady bountiful in every respect! Another, barely eighteen, sat next to me throughout the performance. Mounted upon a table, my only projecting work consisted of adjusting pressure on the spring clutch of the bottom take-up spool below the projector stand. As the spool became heavier with the weight of the film, this take-up required constant attention, especially with a two-and-a-half hour show.

As I slowly moved the adjustment with my left hand, the other slowly slipped beneath the girl's dress to caress a smooth thigh atop of her stockings.. This girl attracted me as no other, and I looked forward to these Thursday show-dates. One week during the inky darkness of a thriller we cuddled and kissed in a wild manner. I knew she would stay behind after the show allowing us the freedom to carry on regardless. Unfortunately, her younger sister arrived for the girl to take her home after attending a child's birthday party.

The following week a thick-set man approached me while I was threading up the machine. He tapped my shoulder. "I'll tell you this once only, mate. If I hear of you touching my wife again, it will be my pleasure to re-arrange your face permanently!"

At Silverstone Church Hall twenty massively built men from the timber yards paid for their tickets asking the well-worn question "What time does the serial go on?" When the feature ran over 100 minutes the only support was the serial. After the trailers when the feature was barely under way these men made considerable noise leaving their chairs in a scramble for the exit. Enquiring about this odd behaviour I was told repeatedly, "We're losing valuable drinking time at the pub, mate. Serials are the best part. Smashing!"

During Holy Week when the Vicar refused permission for the hall to be used for shows, Columbia allowed a chapter to be retained for the next week. A double helping of mindless soap! Many complaints from the beer-drinking men, "Grief. Me arse is bloody numb! Sitting all this time on a hard chair. Why not show a whole serial for one night?" Shades of Baghdad. Fifteen episodes at twenty minutes each. A cinematic marathon!

During the light evenings locations needed blacking out, especially Creaton where the summer sun's rays fell upon eight windows. If a patron caught against a curtain a shaft of brilliant sunshine upset the performance. I carried bundles of dark curtaining materials obtained cheaply from various second-hand shops and jumble sales which filled the side-car daily. At least they helped pad my equipment saving hot lamps and warm valves from the shocks produced by bumpy roads, especially country lanes riddled with large pot-holes. Blacking-out each location consumed a good deal of time in preparation, and, after the show, removing the curtains and old wooden panels some halls retained from the war years was hard work.

In the hot months of June and July I enjoyed a pleasing sight—viewing a sunset—a rare event for me. Upstairs in the box, in any season of the year, one never saw a sunset. Frequently I motored home on the reliable B.S.A. motor-cycle deep-breathing and admiring silhouetted trees in many glorious sunsets. My thoughts often turned to Bob imprisoned in the poky box of the old Regal consuming his bag of chips during the last, late showing of a long hot day. By ten-thirty in the evening, I would walk my parent's dog around a nearby park after a successful village show, realising Bob had just changed-over projectors for the final double reel.

Were we eccentrics choosing to work over hot arcs for long hours in the airless confines of a box? Many people work at jobs others despised because they loved it. So we projectionists all those years ago: men who had pride in their work. Showmanship! Fading down the house lights so slowly patrons scarcely noticed the approaching darkness, leaving the soft coloured tabs which burst apart as the music record faded away, and the sub-title melody faded in. Each credit for the feature had a different colour mix from the battens and foots until all faded out as the director's name faded from view.

Reality! Surely nothing reminds the picture-goer how unreal a scene is when some young inexperienced director introduces slow motion into an action scene. Have none of these wonder boys ever studied Orson Welles? Do cinemas have projectionists or mere operators trained to make-up reels, press buttons, and nothing more? Yes, we loved the job, often working against the clock, not employed in a mindless, repetitious factory job, wishing away the hours until finishing time.

To be a mobile showman was to enjoy a satisfying worthwhile life; meeting the public and hearing of their various difficulties. Farmers, smallholders, village handymen, window cleaners, parish councillors, ladies from the Women's Institute. Women who were with the W.V.S. did so much throughout the war. Shivering from Scotland's icy blast, as one left the night train, one knew that the ladies working through the night produced soup, dried egg, and beans on toast. I would notice many mature ladies entering my various venues who had been through the war years enjoying the films of Bette Davis, Clark Gable, and Spencer Tracy—all similar to Mrs. Green at the Plaza matinees all those years ago. Occasional snatches of conversation, "Lost her son in the navy." "Never been the same since her husband died in that tractor accident."

All right! So it's the fabric of human nature, in all walks of life people paying to be entertained and rewarding for the entertainer. Little wonder that thespians prefer performing to a live audience than before a camera. Every village performance was different as regards the audience reaction.

Apart from the work involved in darkening halls, the summer months brought a distinct drop in revenue, yet my profit always gave me twice the average wage.

With my change of luck with the dropping of entertainment tax, life was to change completely in 1949. I met my cousin's friend the ladies' hairdresser again—a real strawberry blonde: natural, no dyed locks here! Lois possessed shoulder-length burnished gold hair, not red. Her customers thought it was dyed. It tumbled about her shoulders, framing a beautiful face with sweet dimples. At twenty-five, with many wild oats distantly behind me, I decided somehow I would do anything to try and take her out somewhere sometime. My last overture in this direction failed miserably, and this time I almost ordered her to meet me. "I'll take you to the pictures. Not in a town cinema. Oh, no! My private cinema Sunday evening You'll come, won't you? I know you will." She agreed.

Each Sunday evening with the projector operating through the open kitchen doorway a rehearsal was given on a screen across the piano in the lounge. We managed to seat eight people: my parents, sister, and several neighbours. This performance was the highlight of the week for all concerned, long before television.

Columbia's product produced excellent business at the villages. The 16mm. hire catalogue contained two Bogarts *(Sahara*[70] and *Dead Reckoning*[71]), with Fred Astaire and Rita Hayworth musicals *You'll Never Get Rich* [72] and *You Were Never Lovelier,*[73] plus many two-reel comedies including *The Three Stooges;* very popular on the circuit.

Lois sat beside me in the kitchen as the B.T-H. rattled through a double-feature of *The Devil Bat*[74] and *Meet Boston Blackie.*[75] Bela Lugosi's career was going down in the former, yet his performance thrilled Lois, who gripped my hand for almost seventy minutes! We became inseparable and the following week she travelled on the pillion to the villages; except Friday, her late night at the hairdressers.

Life was wonderful. She took the cash and issued tickets, giving me the freedom to seat patrons and listen to their views regarding films and stars. Despite the age of Columbia's features, all were

---

[70] 1942 Zoltan Korda
[71] 1947 John Cromwell
[72] 1941 Sidney Lanfield
[73] 1942 Wm Seiter
[74] 1941 Jean Yarborough
[75] 1941 Jean Yarborough

action-packed and ideal for my circuit. Lois would stay beside the machine while I attended to various problems with juvenile patrons. Two locations had lavatories situated to the side of the stage, and children, bored in love scenes, frequently ran in and out of them. This created much noise and by leaving the doors open they caused shafts of light to fall across the screen. Also, they chattered loudly during dialogue scenes, and, no longer a one-man band, I was able to deal with this quietly and efficiently when Lois was with me.

Drawbacks to road showing were only overcome by first-hand experience. Hall light-switches yards away from the projector; mains switch-gear requiring cable to be run behind the last row of chairs; often no parking adjacent to the hall; during wet weather it was difficult to unload electrical equipment, and so on. At least in those far-off days no-one tampered with the combination. Vandalism did not exist.

Lois' presence helped me to provide a professional touch to the travelling cinema. My days spent dating local girls were over. Love life for projectionists was grim with regard to meeting the opposite sex. Usherettes, like barmaids were spoiled for choice by scores of admirers. I never learned to dance, and while my friends cuddled up to girls, usually on the back row, like all my contemporaries, I worked the box. After the two years void of female company while abroad, suddenly girls were available in town and especially the country. One girl tried claiming me as the father for her obvious pregnancy. Meeting Lois changed all this. Apart from the village shows we spent most Saturdays in London seeing many notable productions. Sundays, she stayed for tea, and joined me in the kitchen where we kissed madly throughout the film show as everyone in the lounge gazed at the screen.

One evening after loading the side-car carefully outside the Nissen hut cinema at Roade, a man approached me; in his mid-forties, dressed in tweeds. His pair of golden retrievers sniffed the motor-cycle tyres and bounded about the field. We had enjoyed a long conversation, when he quietly said, "Nice to meet an ex-serviceman showing some initiative operating his own business in the days of this socialist nanny state. I've heard you were running cinema shows on my land. I'm Wake of Courteenhall. People hereabouts call me Major Wake, though I'm not keen on keeping up my army rank now that that's all behind us."

I recalled hearing in detail at school, where I was in Wake House, the history of the Hereward Wake family spanning the centuries. He invited me to arrange a film show to entertain his tenant farmer workers at Courteenhall House in mid-October.

"A harvest home film show. How about it?"

A Saturday date was agreed, and I promised to send him a catalogue from which to choose a film. Only days later I returned from Filmhire after buying spare lamps for the B.T-H., late for lunch after hearing of Smithies' hard-working week which embraced projector repairs and operating five children's parties.

Mother was excited. "I thought you'd never come. You have a visitor. Lord Wake, I think. He's in the front room."

"Ah! Northover. I've called to see these film lists. Hardly ever visit cinemas, but my sister and the ladies at Couteenhall can choose a film. Your mother gave me these to study."

He finished a cup of tea. "I see the average film is hired for a fiver. So let the ladies choose and I'll pay £15. Make a tenner for you. O.K.?"

I gulped and nodded approval. "I must go. Thank your mother for the tea, and do enjoy your lunch which smells delicious. Stew, if I'm not mistaken."

* * * * *

Bob insisted on helping with the show, and brought his record player to ensure a professional performance. We both enjoyed tea in the stables. These had been converted into nice living accommodation, for Courteenhall baronial hail looked vast and imposing, yet too expensive to heat, the Major explained.

They had chosen *Escape* to *Happiness*,[76] a lovely film, starring Leslie Howard and Ingrid Bergman, but with a poor sound-track on variable area. Were it not for Bob's additional amplifier, many dialogue scenes would have been inaudible I insisted Bob received £3 from the fee.

When the cheque arrived I presented it to the National Provincial Bank. The teller gave me a strange look, and asked me to wait. A few minutes later the manager greeted me with a puzzled expression.

"This cheque is drawn on the Wakes' special account, and is payable to Midgetone Mobile Movies, A. E. Northover. Have you a bank account?"

---

[76] a.k.a. Intermezzo 1939 David Selznick: Gregory Ratoff, the actor, directing.

I shook my head as he gave me three five-pound notes.

"Do consider us. We are bankers for the Lord Rank. J. Arthur Rank, you know."

I was thankful that he didn't walk to the door with me to see the mud-splattered combination outside with the words *Midgetone Mobile Film Shows* along the side-car.

Lois' parents owned a motor garage showroom. Her father was not impressed with my mobile work, especially driving around in all weathers with Lois on the pillion.

"Not a proper business, is it? Very precarious method of making a few pounds. Cinemas! Never cared for them!"

My explanations to allay his fears appeared unconvincing.

"You need to look around for a decent job. Get yourself a car. Give this sort of thing up. We think a great deal of Lois, you know. Think about it."

His objections fell upon deaf ears. At last my own cinema operated nicely and proved lucrative. A terrific sense of well-being existed as I arrived at a village where groups of children watched me unload with cries of "It's the Picture Man!"

* * * * * * *

10: A Socialist Heaven

At my suggestion, in 1950 Lois purchased a ladies' hairdressing business above an auctioneer's premises in the town centre. A going concern since 1932, in spite of a lease renewable every three months, the place priced at only £450 plus a mere 30/- weekly rent was a bargain. Her pay of £4 weekly increased to £20 within a few weeks. We became lotus-eaters, spending our joint income of over £40 weekly on London visits, expensive clothes, and dining-out in style.

Smithy and Jacko, as they were affectionately known, soldiered on at Filmhire Ltd. Both earning only £12 weekly between them they helped me considerably; always willing to lend for a few shillings over two hours of films catalogued at a fiver. I suspect this went into their own pockets, and I did not blame them for these occasional odd amounts.

Over fifty projectors had been sold to schools, and through the incompetence of the various operators they were inundated with servicing work. I learned B.T-H. had advised two modifications to the 301: to dispense with the cumbersome sprocket which encircled the revolving sound drum, and to alter the lamphouse to receive 750w. lamps—the brilliant Bob Munn had beaten their boffins by many months, much to my satisfaction!

The county engaged a road safety officer in the person of the excitable Italian Mr. Valvona. His job was to show safety-first documentaries to town and county institutions, and I met him several times at Filmhire. "No sound! Nothing! Projector impossible!" he raved amid wild gestures.

Here I must describe the worst feature of the 301 sound system. When fitting a new exciter lamp, when locating the bayonet-style pins, if one pressed the lamp down unduly between the brass holding strips, it could not be retrieved until the machine had been dismantled completely. This meant that the housing had to be removed, the amplifier unscrewed, and then the lamp retrieved and replaced. When focusing the exciter, the leads wore thin and became distorted due to the heat. I always dropped a blob of solder on the connecting end, filing this flat. In addition, the filament sagged after a few hours of use, requiring constant re-focusing.

One can imagine the trouble in store for Smithy and Jacko. Often there were six projectors awaiting service with attached labels – No Sound!

We've just had a visit from Mr. Valvona," wailed Smithy.

"No sound?" I suggested.

"Up to our ears in work!" Jacko explained. "So far, Smithy has run four evening shows – kid's parties."

"And for no extra pay!" moaned his colleague. Can't you take on a few private parties at weekends and help us out? We dread Christmas."

"Christmas!" Smithy explained. "Ye Gods! I'll go spare." I agreed to help out whenever possible. The fee for a show, averaging an hour, was £10, and with the films costing only £1 it was a licence to print money, I thought.

Setting-up in the lounges of rich people was easy; there was no need for Bob's extra amplifier, or the large non-stop spools. The children were fascinated watching me preparing for projection, observing in awe as I threaded up, and their excited little fingers made designs in the beam as I switched on to line-up on the screen. For an hour of peace the mothers washed-up, and returned to watch the final twenty minutes of the programme. As an *encore* I would rewind the final short and project it again. Apparently my show was cheaper and less trouble than the one-man clown and magician shows!

"The magician needed adults to help with tricks. You've been a god-send. Absolute peace for over an hour!" became a familiar accolade. It proved a lucrative and most satisfying experience until I made the 'big time'.

"You don't know what it's like, running a show for a large party", cried Smithy.

Yes! I made the 'big time'—a show at a working-men's club for an audience of two hundred screaming children between the ages of three and fourteen. An absolute NIGHTMARE.

One soaking-wet Saturday afternoon I spent half-an-hour unloading equipment from the combination, which could only be parked a hundred yards from the venue. Once I was inside, wet-headed and breathless, a large matron grabbed my left hand as I tried drying my hair with a handkerchief.

"Where on earth have you been? Get this show going at once!"

"It's only 3.30. I understand the performance is due to start at 4.30," I complained.

"Leave George alone, Jill! Adam, don't do that. It's not nice!" Several under-fives were opening a can of film. "Put it down!" I cried.

"If I have to tell you again, Sylvia Johnson, you'll go home. Do you understand? Leave him alone. David, stop encouraging her," she shouted over the din created by groups of children running about yelling and shouting. In desperation she muttered in an undertone, "See what I mean? Get your show going - now! Don't stand around combing your hair!" Her remarks to the energetic excitable children were like Joyce Grenfell's wonderful monologue, only more emphatic and imperious.

Leaving me she moved swiftly to the rear of the spacious hall, and clapped her hands, yelling at the top of her voice "Quiet. Quiet! Shut up! Be quiet." With her arms waving frantically a measure of silence was achieved. "Right, you kids! Now listen to your Auntie Annie. This man is going to give us a film show."

Cries of: "Do they talk?" "Bet we've seen 'em at the pictures." "Are they in colour?" "Bloody lot of rubbish, I'll bet." Another scream from the brass-throated Auntie Annie, "Shut up! You swear again and out you go, Smith. Now listen to me, Adam. If I have to tell you once more, home you go. That's a filthy habit! This nice man will show films. Cartoon films. Comedy films." (aside) "You do have cartoons?"

I nodded after lifting the 301 from the carrying case. "There you are—cartoons. Perhaps some of you older children can help this nice man." She glared at me red-faced, hair awry, eyes blazing. "Get going – now!" and left the room, quickly disappearing into the kitchen, after instructing the teenagers to remove the trestle tables and arrange the seats. Amid scores of screaming voices and the crash-bang of countless chairs being hurled about I tried to hang the screen.

"'E's got a bed-sheet. Load of rubbish," shouted a boy. As I tried throwing the speaker lead over four girders, everyone cheered. The loudspeaker, propped on a chair beside the screen, rocked precariously as a girl, trying to help, pulled the lead, handing it to me, "Here's the end, mister."

"Quick! One of you hold the speaker - please!" I yelled. The projector seemed dangerously at risk atop of the stand, erected on a table (the only one available, with swaying legs, removed from the kitchen as some ten women complained they needed it for trays containing half-eaten plates of sandwiches and jelly trifle).

I resorted to lighting a cigarette, in an unsuccessful attempt to calm my nerves, while leaving the projector to connect the extension lead to the mains supply. While I was threading-up furiously, the noise of the children reached a crescendo of shouts and screams; several young boys were fist-fighting, small girls were crying, and teenage boys grouped themselves round attractive girls of the same age. One lad, who told me to extinguish my cigarette, was lighting several and giving them to girls.

Generally, the commotion was so loud I couldn't hear the familiar 'plop' from the speaker when I flicked a match-stick over the exciter-lamp beam. Suddenly, someone switched off the hall lighting. Before I could object, it was restored. Thankfully, I started the 301, which caused a roar of approval. As each short ended, the lights were switched on once more. When all the films had ended no-one could locate the switch and an uproar ensued, with boys switching the lights on and off.

"What a lot of rubbish!" a young girl told me.

"Is this the end?" shouted a tall boy.

After re-packing the projector I hastened to the kitchen for 'Auntie Annie'. "All done? Right, my old man'll pay you when he comes from work. He's on overtime."

We returned to the hall, where two boys were undoing the screen cords tied to chairs. As I climbed a wobbling ladder to take down the lantern sheet, 'Auntie' was announcing further party details, "My old—I mean Uncle Jack will be here very soon to present prizes for the games, so no more shouting or rude remarks to your Auntie Annie!"

"You're not our aunt, you old trout!" cried a boy. 'Auntie' breathed-in deeply, her ample bosom swelling to tremendous proportions.

"That does it! Any moment Uncle Jack will take over," she glared at the heckler, "and he can be very disagreeable, as you all know. So watch out the lot of you. Remember what happened to Tony Foster on the Blackpool train trip last year?" This last remark produced a hush from everyone. I could only smile to myself concerning the dire consequences which befell Master Foster.

I really do believe that if the writer T.E.B. Clarke, who was responsible for many famous Ealing comedies, had created a script about a mobile cinema showman, the laughter induced would have matched that for *The Ladykillers* and others of that *genre*.

* * * * *

In contrast with the above, a very subdued private film show followed a few months later, at Wilbye Grange, the home of local businessman Mr. Norman, who owned several high-class bread and pastry shops in the Wellingborough area. He was an avid lover of jazz, owning a vast collection of timpani which he played with much expertise before the film performance.

Syd Field's widow was present, to watch two 1,600' reels featuring her husband. The prints, in pristine condition, were posted to me, registered, direct from the Wardour St. labs.

Lois accompanied me, and we found the evening extremely sad. Field's fame came late in his lifetime in show-business striving for stardom in films. Excerpts for showing came from *London Town* made by Rank in 1946 and directed by the American Wesley Ruggles. Mrs. Field complained the music hall sequences appeared out-of-place and old hat, and the script contained few laughs.

This was intended as the first British musical to equal the Warner, Fox, and MGM extravaganzas. This failed because British films suffered from a lack of choreographers who did not produce a dance sequence for ten minutes based on a three-minute song: like the music arrangers. Unfortunately, the native industry never employed the talents of Busby Berkeley or Bob Fosse—the latter's expertise in the 1953 production of *Kiss Me Kate* was outstanding[77].

The second offering was from *Cardboard Cavalier,* directed by Walter Forde, which Syd made opposite Margaret Lockwood. This, too, failed to make him an international star, and both productions failed miserably at the box office. Apparently, Mrs Fields had never watched either production, so it was a 'first night' tinged with recriminations and tears.

* * * * *

During the Christmas of 1950, my step-brother Jack, an ex-Desert Rat from the African campaign, was invalided from the army developing T.B., becoming a patient at Creaton Sanatorium, where my father had stayed for almost a year before my birth. A local well-meaning vicar borrowed an old 16mm. Gebescope, and hired a programme from Filmhire to give a Christmas film show for the patients. This was abandoned after a mere twenty minutes due to the lamp failing. Without a spare, everyone was disappointed.

Arranging to hold a Columbia programme for an extra Saturday, I gave a free show at the sanatorium. Obviously, the films had played at the local village hall that same week, where several of the staff had

---

[77] M.G.M. (George Sydney) Choreographer: Hermes Pan Music: Cole Porter Musical Director: André Previn

attended on Wednesday. In a letter of thanks from Dr. Starkey, the consultant chest physician, was an invitation to present a weekly date for a suitable fee. We agreed £6—without a hall fee, and having to take the cash at the door, this show in a small 50-seater concert hall was most enjoyable. I set up the equipment on stage to form a 'box' behind the thick velour house tabs, opened a fraction to allow for the projector beam and my view. Matron met me each Tuesday with a plate of tea and biscuits!

One foggy evening she did not expect me: I assured her a motor-cycle combination 'ate' fog and that I never missed a show date.

"This is all very well, but so dangerous for you—and my patients. You've risked this journey for nothing. I cannot allow them to walk from wards to here in this penetrating fog."

At my suggestion, I set-up in a ward containing twenty beds. In the centre were some thirty chairs for up-patients who entered via corridors. However, this instant ward cinema created another, much worse, problem: it was open. Not under lock and key as mental institutions, but literally open one side to the elements. Fog swirled inside, the up-patients wore overcoats to keep warm, and I was frozen throughout the hour-and-threequarter show, even though it was shortened by omitting the serial! I kept my hands reasonably warm by holing them above the lamphouse. The applause at the end of *Cover Girl* was most embarrassing. Entertaining another twenty bed-patients meant there was no return to the luxury of the concert hall.

Within weeks, a letter arrived from the hospital management committee, asking me to operate weekly at two other Northampton hospitals for the same fee, including two performances each evening for the additional show-dates. This placed me in a quandary. Public or hospital Showman? With takings assured I decided to operate the three hospitals weekly.

* * * * * * *

11: Inside Locations Looking Out

Bob Munn frowned at my decision to take on the hospitals, "I think it's risky, Arth., dropping three good public dates. Especially using Creaton Village Hall for Wednesdays. It's the worst take of the week, only averages a fiver." Bob thought my news about a hospital circuit disappointing, and he noticed my surprise.

I lit a cigarette and handed one to him. "Yes, I suppose so. Being barely a quarter-mile from the san. it's so easy to set up afterwards in readiness for the following night. Obviously, no carrying of equipment to and from home."

"Just laziness, Arth. Business-wise it's a let-down. Another thing. Why charge only £7 for two shows nightly, twice weekly? Should be six pounds per show plus four more for the extra performance. An extra pound doesn't make sense: you're only saving the hall fees! It's risky. Have you got a contract?"

"No contract," I told him, "Just a gentleman's agreement like the one with Columbia."

He pinched out the cigarette, and placed the stub-end into a small tin. "Do for a quick drag between reels! I know a small family business run by two brothers. Served hospitals with greens, fruit, veg. Packed up a country round. Wasn't long before the hospitals suddenly changed suppliers. I've heard of several mobile cinemas in the area: Mumford & Cooknell pack the town hall on Fridays at Thame, and another company, Banbury Cine Sound, do well. It'll be difficult to find five locations again. A competitor'll jump in!"

I shrugged my shoulders and believed twenty-three pounds weekly was regular bread-and-butter, including the lean summer months, as the remaining locations should make up a reasonable living.

The government was engaged in setting up the national Health Service, and for several months I received no payments. February's invoice was paid at the end of March. The remaining locations covered the cost of film rentals and travelling expenses. Due to possessing little in savings I was obliged to borrow from my parents, with board suspended for over seven weeks. Mother remarked my finances would be hopeless, were I married and paying a mortgage.

"Marriage—that's a question. Do you plan to live together using the spare room at the back of the hairdressing shop for ever?" she enquired. "I'm certain her parents expect you to marry."

Strange as it may appear, Lois and I never once discussed the subject. We decided to become engaged during the summer of 1951. Her father was unimpressed with my track record as a businessman.

"I never made a proper profit until I employed another pair of hands and paid for someone else's sweat. While I worked on a car, running indoors and out to serve petrol, I lost car sales. Yours isn't a business as such. If you'd any sense about you, you'd employ someone to operate cinema shows for children and the hospitals while you carry on with the public shows. As for Lois, she'll not wish to work in hairdressing for ever! She'll want a family. Just look at the pair of you! A flat for thirty bob a week, take a bus to your mother's for Sunday lunch, visit us for tea! Saturdays in London! Total irresponsibility in my book!"

The hospital exhibitions presented problems. On Monday evening I operated in the terminally-ill old folk's ward at St. Edmund's hospital, which only a few years previously had been the workhouse. Using a wheeled stretcher I transported the equipment using a lift, down two flights of stairs, and into the huge glass-windowed day-room. Here, as I hung the screen, the small motor rewound the large reel, watched intently by a group of mentally-retarded folk of both sexes and varying ages. Ill-dressed, one noticed many of them on the streets, and this large, gloomy place was their home.

One man in his early sixties, well-built, broad-shouldered, and dressed in a threadbare black suit, wore a huge cloth cap pulled down over his hair and forehead. I recalled seeing him seated on the front row of the Regal many times. He guffawed loudly in quiet scenes, often warned to be quiet by the manager. "I'm Texas, 'cos I come from there. I'll 'elp you, mister picture man. You just call me Tex."

His mental age was roughly ten years, yet he lifted projector and speaker in each massive arm as though they were a pair of oranges. I felt so sorry for him, poor lost soul—and so many more. Some young girls were obviously pregnant and evidently retarded. They would watch me and giggle as I threaded up.

"This is Polly, mister. She's in love with you. Want to do her, mister?"

A small thin girl with large eyes smiled at me: the grin of a simpleton some despicable devil had impregnated. The medical superintendent occasionally entered to check all was well; as in Dickens' novels everyone called him "Master", and moved away swiftly from the projection table as he approached.

My instructions were to show only 'U' certificated films; no heavy drama or mysteries. Many bookings, being unsuitable, created much work and loss of money. Special two-hour shows required make-up and pack-up each week for this location. Filmhire rescued me to supply twelve reels for thirty shillings.

Another difficulty each week presented itself with two shows at the long-term orthopaedic hospital. No lifts, and without Tex to help, I alternated the ladies' ward and children's ward, ending at the men's ward for an 8.30 start. As at St. Edmund's, the first show commenced at 5.30. At least here all was ground level to rush along corridors with a loaded wheeled stretcher.

It was the men's ward which proved troublesome. Twelve patients who, while appreciating the film show, wanted to club together and hire films of their choosing, as programmes suitable for village work were quickly frowned upon after a few weeks.

"Oh, no! Not another George Formby? How about *The Red Shoes*"? "*Citizen Kane*?" etc. etc.

One evening I fell against the side of the lift at S. Edmund's hospital, pulling the speaker from the trolley. Tex saved it from crashing upon my up-turned face. As I looked up, he grinned at me, "All O.K. picture man? No 'arm done." For a brief moment I shuddered, recalling Herbert without a cap gazing down at me a lifetime ago.

We parted company eventually, and he cried. Bob's warning was correct. I submitted a list of forthcoming bookings to the secretary of the management committee, only to receive a terse reply: "Cinema exhibitions are being arranged by another film company from January next."

Nothing more, nothing less.

Tex was badly upset. He bit a lip when I gave him a tin of fifty smokes. "Do for Christmas, Tex."

He looked at the tin, held it high, and sobbed bitterly, quickly waving his arms about madly and striking the tin on the table to attract attention.

"This is the end. 'E ain't coming no more, the picture man. 'E don't mind us making noises an' laughing at pictures. No! No! 'E just ain't going to come anymore. No more picture man."

* * * * *

It was difficult to arrange locations and prepare an annual block-booking with Columbia. Most of their well-known features had been screened, and the majority of shorts. Deciding to shop elsewhere only resulted in extra fees. Catalogues from Associated British, Twentieth Century-Fox, and Paramount arrived regularly by post, but, apart from the price, many were too long. Allowing for the twenty-minute serial, a feature of almost two hours was out of the question.

Arriving late for lunch one morning, after calling at Filmhire, I found a large car was parked outside the house, next to my combination.

"Someone to see you, very overpowering, from Metro. He's in the front room—been here half an hour," my mother explained.

Strewn over the settee were several quad posters and a larger leather briefcase crammed with documents. On the sideboard, a black homburg hat, a plate of biscuits, and a cup of tea.

"Ah! Mr. Northover. At last! We are M.G.M." exclaimed a balding thickset man attired in an expensive pin-striped suit. We shook hands.

"Sloman of M.G.M. The company you cannot ignore. Offering your good self the cream of film productions and the world's greatest stars. I gather you've been road-showing for some time, and never approached us. Not good business! We know your difficulties because we have twenty vans on the road throughout the southern counties."

I mentioned my association with Columbia, and wisely he made no effort to criticize a competitor.

"Operated by Harry Cohn direct from Hollywood, frequently visits their London office. They have looked after you well, my boy? But you need our product. Must have it. Essential! I'm not here to sell you our fine films. Not at all. Just a courtesy visit. Here to help. You have just one unit on the road? These posters I'll leave with you, and our contract, which must be agreed when we make deals in the future.[78] Your mother tells me you've been involved with local hospitals. Known as shut-in locations, such as ships at sea, prisons, and so forth, where no bars apply. You have shown the latest releases, naturally?"

He became alarmed on hearing that the films were anything other than new releases.

---

[78] M.G.M's contract consisted of six foolscap pages on thick heavy paper, with the inevitable lion motif above paragraphs of confusing legal jargon: whereas, heretofore, the party of the first part, and the party of the second and third parties—all very confusing. Over half-an-hour's reading matter.

"My boy! Dear, dear, dear!" he said, glancing at my list of recent bookings. "Such very old titles. Why most of them are productions from the 40s! Such tired old product! Poor pictures indeed for hospital patients. What do you charge?"

"Ten pound a show," I lied. Somehow I dared not admit the actual fee, and felt thankful. He pressed an arm about my shoulder.

"My boy! Ten pounds! Unbelievable! The average rate for 'shut-ins' is twenty-five. Nationwide! In some instances we ourselves charge thirty. Oh, dear me. Dear, dear, dear! You ought to have come to us for advice. Brand-new releases for your shows, before appearing at local cinemas in many instances. Columbia failed to advise you? Unforgivable!"

I dared not explain the twice-nightly shows for an extra pound, and felt foolish. He paced up and down the room for a moment.

"Do excuse me, please," he said, pulling back a curtain and peering into the street. "There's an old motor-cycle contraption near my vehicle. Probably belongs to some teenage tearaway. Don't want him driving off and maybe scratching my car!"

He closed the briefcase, retrieved his hat, and extended a hand.

"I must go. Study our new releases. Get in touch when you feel ready to do a deal."

We shook hands once more, and he departed. Studying his embossed-lettered card with a crinkled gold edge, I rubbed my chin thoughtfully, remembering a letter received in Iraq from Gaumont-British. I found it in my filing cabinet and carefully read a paragraph—

> *There are many aspects to consider before commencing a mobile cinema circuit. For example, your locations must be over three miles distant from 35mm. cinemas. Never book films in advance, known as 'block booking'. Obviously, since films are over a year after release before appearing on 16mm., many will be two years old at the end of a block booking. Do not exhibit old feature films, but use up-to-date ones the public will wish to see. If showing at 'shut-in' locations, always be advised by a reputable renter, who can supply new releases currently showing on general release.*

Signed by the general sales manager, this advice made much sense. Ignored by my excited attitude over the lifting of entertainment tax, I had rushed in where fools would not tread.

After the M.G.M. contact, mother re-iterated her frequent objection to the choice of films, especially those shown at hospitals.

"I've said every Sunday for weeks about how old the films were. All very good you praising this film or that because you enjoyed it during the war, but 1941 is ten years ago, and young teenagers find this completely out-of-date. I enjoyed *Love From A Stranger,*[79] and Cary Grant appeared in his early twenties *in The Amazing Quest of Ernest Bliss* [80] made over twenty years ago. I think this is the reason that you've lost the hospitals."

All too late, I booked recent releases including *The Third Man* [81] from G-B., four Associated British productions plus *Pathé News*, albeit a week old. A few editions of the news were much appreciated by bed patients at the sanatorium, which gave graphic sequences of the Wembley cup final, a month or two before winding-up hospital work.

The local Labour party wrote to me from the village of Broughton, three miles north of Kettering, asking for a quote to present a public weekly show-date. They would hire the hall and issue tickets for their funds. I quoted seven pounds, which they considered reasonable.

My weekly circuit now consisted of the following

Mon	Harpole Band Institute	£ 5 0 0
Tuesday	Silverstone Church Hall	£ 8 0 0
Wed	Creaton Village Hall	£ 4 0 0
Thurs	Hanslope Church Hall (Bucks)	£10 0 0
Fri	Broughton Village Hall	£ 7 0 0

In addition I commenced a monthly performance at yet another T.B. hospital, Rushden Sanatorium, on the last Saturday evening of the month, the films being most recent, and carefully selected.

The £34 weekly average takings, much reduced than before the advent of the hospital circuit, and all with increased hall fees, and film rental and travelling costs, only produced a profit of a bare £12 weekly. 'Bus services were cheaper and more reliable for country folk, and with many more activities available—dances, keep-fit evenings, bingo nights—the weekly film shows were not the attraction of yesteryear.

* * * * *

At Christmas 1951 I gave a show for Lois' parents and relatives. Purchasing an excellent Kodak 16mm. cine camera from Filmhire, I amused a festive gathering by showing candid shots of the family.

---

[79] 1936 G-B. Trafalgar Films: Roland V. Lee
[80] 1936 G-B.: Alfred Zeidler
[81] 1949: Carol Reed

The camera, in mint condition, came complete with case and spare drive belt, and was made in 1924, the year of my birth. During this period, tape recorders were all the rage, with a repetitious joke where people heard their voices played back, unwittingly recorded as they arrived. Seeing themselves for the first time, especially in candid shots, produced a great deal of fun.

In May 1952 we married. A quiet planned affair culminated in a church ceremony, plus a reception for over a hundred guests. The event was filmed on 16mm. black-and-white by Lou Warwick, the local newspaper columnist 'Hamtune', cine photography being his hobby. Smithy and Jacko had suggested I contact him with a view to the filming. Due to poor light indoors, most of the reception creates smiles when projected, because Lou filmed at a mere six frames per second, resulting in almost double-speed action for several feet!

During May I used four bookings from M.G.M., and lost money on three. Only the remake of *King Solomon's Mines* attracted patrons.[82]

After the lovely summer months of that year, trade fell to a depressing level. I used programmes from Filmhire at only three pounds for the five shows. A Laurel and Hardy double-feature bill of *Sons of the Desert* [83] and *Way Out West* [84] did wonderful business, even though both had been previously projected, with supporting shorts, at all locations. The winter began in a promising fashion, but declined badly in January 1953. Friday evenings for the Labour party afforded sufficient profit to provide a Christmas party for invalid O.A.Ps., yet a summer outing planned for July appeared doubtful, due to extremely small profits.

Everything was in decline. Renters required more rental in tandem with village hall committees increasing charges. Projector lamps at six pounds gave little value for money, as the filaments quickly sagged producing poor light, and the quality did not improve over the years.

I doubted that takings would hold up to provide any kind of a reasonable living. In every respect, the mobile days were collapsing rapidly.

* * * * * * *

---

[82] 1952 M.G.M.
[83] 1937: Hal Roach Stan Laurel producing James Horne
[84] 1936: Hal Roach a.k.a. 'Fraternally Yours'

MIDGETONE MOBILE CINEMAS OF NORTHAMPTON
EACH WEEK AT THIS HALL ON WEDNESDAYS... AT 7.30 p.m. DOORS 7.15

MAY CINEMA PROGRAMMES

TROUBLE IN THE FORMBY BREWERY—A RIOT OF FUN!

GEORGE FORMBY GOOGIE WITHERS

TROUBLE BREWING

EPISODE 2 of "JUNIOR G-MEN OF THE AIR", Etc.

SHOWING ON :— MAY 7.

M-G-M's BIG MERRY MIRTHQUAKE MUSICAL—IT HAS EVERYTHING!

ABBOTT & COSTELLO

RIO RITA

SERIAL Ep. 3 INTEREST

SHOWING ON :— MAY 14.

BIG ACTION WESTERN

THE RANGEBUSTERS

FUGITIVE VALLEY

ALSO GRAND MYSTERY THRILLER

TOM NEAL PAMELA BLAKE

HATBOX MYSTERY

SERIAL Ep. 4

SHOWING ON :— MAY 21

M-G-M's MIGHTY SPECTACLE—THE AFRICAN ADVENTURE WITH A CAST OF THOUSANDS

STEWART GRANGER DEBORAH KERR

KING SOLOMONS MINES

SERIAL Ep. 5

SHOWING ON :— MAY. 28.

OVER 2 HOURS NON-STOP PERFORMANCE • PERFECT SOUND
PERFECT CINEMA-SIZE PICTURE

Prices of Admission: Adults 1/9 • Children 1/– • Pensioners 9d.

All Communications to: 172 WYCLIFFE ROAD, NORTHAMPTON • PARTIES & CLUBS A SPECIALITY

12: Let's *NOT* Go To The Pictures

The rot had set in many months previously, and the premier locations suffered first. Hanslope, in Buckinghamshire, was the best location visited, and the church hall converted into a first-class cinema. The windows possessed full-length black curtains closed by pulling a single cord. Retained from the war years, these helped enhance the sound by cutting the reverberation time of the hall. Through an open door, the projector stood high on a kitchen table, and the throw completely cleared the audience. This kitchen 'box' ensured the 301 merely whirred away out of sight to patrons, and was the only one of my public shows with this luxury. Often, in other places, people would notice the fast spinning of the top reel and disturb other patrons by pulling on coats, preparing to rush out rather than stand for 'The King' trailer. So here, at least, the show appeared professional.

Patrons were quiet, and generally adults out-numbered the children. Many families attended, couples with two children, say, and a good booking resulted in a full house. Parents congratulated me regarding various features.

"It's nice, enjoyable, and we know where our children will be for one evening. Out of town, relying on 'buses, especially with teenagers, can be worrying," was the general impression. A chief inspector of police, whenever free of duty, brought his wife and three children, and declared the regular weekly shows were excellent and good value for money.

For some months we enjoyed an ice-cream interval before the feature. A friend of Bob Munn approached me with a view to selling the product at three venues weekly. In his mid-forties, he brought a teenage girl with him. Sales were reasonable, yet not sufficient to pay for his petrol on many occasions, in my opinion.

Running a month of M.G.M. was successful, and we expected a certain house-full for *King Solomon's Mines* (the Deborah Kerr and Stewart Grainger re-make).[85] Commencing at 7.30 with the serial, the place was not even a third full. Once started, I kept going outside hoping for a last-minute rush. During the break for ices, Lois told me, from the ticket roll numbers, that we were running for £5 3s. 0d. The

[85] M.G.M. 1950: Compton Bennett

amount of ice cream sold was negligible. Once more I glanced into the street: all was extremely quiet. Film rental exceed four pounds, and with the hall fee I knew the evening would be a loss. The poor attendance reminded me of the try-out at Brixworth, when Customs & Excise made more than I did! Several times in the past we were obliged to turn patrons away at Hanslope, and with a film of this calibre expected a busy night.

After packing equipment into the sidecar and preparing to leave, the 80-year old caretaker thanked me for his five shillings – a small gratuity always given.

"Don't worry, my boy, they'll be back next week. You'll see!"

The ice-cream man rarely stayed after the interval.

"That's not his daughter," Lois said, "They were holding hands throughout the feature." It was obviously a romance unknown to his wife, which accounted for these clandestine meetings.

"I thought he looked sheepish when he left," I said. "I won't be a minute, just going to the pub for cigarettes."

Once inside I learned the awful truth—television! The place overflowed with folk with their eyes glued to a small television set on a shelf over the bar. Engrossed with the picture, the publican gave me the wrong change from a pound note, and the wrong brand of cigarette.

"Smashing show. Same as Sunday night. They always repeat Sunday night's programme on Thursdays. Did you see it?"

At Broughton the following evening, trade was subdued. Geoff Cope, the chairman of the local Labour party, said, "It's the telly, Arthur. Quite a few sets now in the village; each week more aerials appear on chimneys. It's surprising how many tellies have been sold since the Coronation. Is there any chance of a reduced fee? Profits have been very poor for weeks now."

Changing the booking list for only the three best locations three days weekly, I used cheap old product from Filmhire and other out-of-town libraries for Mondays and the Friday show, enabling me to charge Broughton only a fiver.

Things were not good at all, and I decided to visit Columbia with a view to a block booking. Here they offered me a situation as a prints manager.

"Both gauges, 35 and 16mm. Good salary, think it over," said Sydney Lomberg, toying with a Biro pen. I offered to take him out to lunch as a snooty secretary entered as if on cue.

"How about sandwiches? Salad or fish?" she asked.

"This is an old client of ours, Miss Peters." I smiled at her as she sniffed and gave me a look as if she had trodden in something bad.

"Lunch? See how it is these days? Never leave the office. Sign of the times," he said with a weak smile.

A three-month block booking at eight pounds for three venues, plus the inevitable serial failed to attract but little business. The word 'television' seemed on everyone's lips. "Did you see this or that?" "Isn't Eamonn Andrews marvellous?" "And MacDonald Hobley." Broadcasters emerged from all sorts of radio shows, becoming TV 'stars' overnight.

In Northampton, as elsewhere, cinemas were having a thin time. Bob left the Regal and on the retirement of the Gaumont chief ran that show with his daughter Lesley as Second. He mentioned the latest innovation for sub-standard film would be 8mm. Apparently the Americans were studying 'sound on 8' seriously. I wondered why the Pathé company didn't re-introduce sound on 9.5mm. They marketed sound films pre-war, and produced a worthwhile projector, the 'Vox', for this gauge.

I gathered Pascoe planned to provide wide-screen presentations at the old Picturedrome, and was most concerned with falling receipts.

"The poor old Roxy is almost ready to close down," Bob said. This, situated close to the station, can be compared to *The Smallest Show on Earth*.[86] Once known as the S. James' Cinema, the place was a large and draughty hall with a corrugated-iron roof, and a horror of a box. A tin hut is the best description, and it contained antiquated Chrono machines, British Acoustic sound, and Eclipse hand-fed arcs. It was freezing cold in winter, with the operators wearing overcoats, and the reverse in summer when swimming trunks were worn. Any piercing screech from railway engines, or trains tearing non-stop through the station, totally drowned the sound system, and heavy storms subdued the sound system as rain poured down on the tin roof!

After it had been on the market for months, attracting no potential buyers, a Nottingham company purchased this down-market place. Behind the cinema, the Dover company carried on business manufacturing wooden lasts for the shoe industry, and the Dover Hall adjoined the Roxy, used throughout the war for a service induction and medical centre. Eventually the property was sold cheaply and

[86] G-B. 1957: Basil Dearden

became a housing development. The Roxy, on the corner of S. James' Road, became the first town cinema to succumb to television fever.

For me, declining receipts in the villages reduced profits to an all-time low. The B.T-H. commenced a Saturday morning children's matinée within the town at a location containing twenty-five windows. A dreadful chore, taking an hour to prepare. Allowing for the monthly sanatorium date and the children's matinée, one week I cleared a profit of exactly £4.00!

As Lois attended to customers in the shop, I sat in the adjoining bed-sitting room boiling a kettle for coffee on a small gas ring, very worried and totally frustrated. Was I living on the profits of her hairdressing? Absolutely! This was my state for many weeks, being subsidised by my wife. Glancing through the Chronicle & Echo, a small panel appeared offering a job selling advertising space for them.

Changing into my best suit I applied and secured the post. The pay, at nine pounds weekly, was better than trying to manage on the meagre profits from the cinema. Explaining to the managing editor I needed to continue showing at Hanslope and Silverstone until the serial concluded, he raised no objection. I decided to operate the monthly hospital performance, and he advised me to show the returns on my income tax form, unconcerned with my evening activities once monthly.

For some weeks I block-booked with a firm in Coventry who were both reliable and cheap, although the product was chiefly pre-war. Contacting Columbia to retain a serial for a reasonable price, I received a terse reply from the Sydney Lomberg office—

> *A deal is not possible for a serial. The charge for twice-weekly hire will be £5. Incidentally, Mr. Lomberg is no longer with this office.*
>
> *Yours truly,*
> *S. Peters (Miss)*
> *Sales Manager*

It turned out that Lomberg had left Columbia for M.G.M. So, strange to believe, I paid more for the 'soap' reel than I did for the programme! With only five more chapters to run, I would close the tabs on my mobile career forever, once it finished. Stupid to continue, yet I didn't wish to break faith with the children who accounted for the bulk of my audience.

The previous five years' work found me in various situations, meeting different people, with no dull moments, and I would wrap it up with few regrets. The log, meticulously kept, covered some four thousand running hours. Over the years the mobile visited Hartwell, Ashton, Silverstone, Creaton, Spratton, Harpole, Broughton, Walgrove, and other one-night try-outs, plus four hospitals. Twenty-two children's parties were given!

Film shows quickly finished at home on Sunday evenings due to television. In-laws preferred watching the box, and tired of seeing themselves on film. The novelty was finished.

* * * * *

Harold Pascoe looked ill when we met down town one morning as I visited local stores for newspaper advertisements. His rotund figure appeared shrunk, and ill-fitting clothes hung loosely about him.

"I'm not covering expenses. You can move to another village, but for me there's nothing to be done. I believe both of my shows will have to close," he told me.

Explaining my new situation he said, "You're better out of the business. The best has gone for ever."

He climbed aboard a 'bus which drove away in seconds. I never saw him again. The de Luxe closed in 1956 and the 'Drome two years later. He died shortly afterwards.

With an advertising colleague I visited the old de Luxe in 1954 for the local second-run of *The Ladykillers.*[87] The film played to rows of empty seats. Only twelve people attended the early evening performance.

Ex-members of the Repertory Theatre made guest appearances in various plays. As they were not averse to publicity, many advertising features were arranged as an entire page of broadsheet covered in photos depicting the star in local shops, posing while trying on shoes or dresses, with suitable captions below the pictures. Freda Jackson, fresh from her British film success, *No Room at the Inn*,[88] was the first star I accompanied around the town.

We selected a shop of each trade, a hairdresser's, restaurant, florist, and so forth. Selling space in such features proved easy with advertisers queuing to take part.

The New Theatre booked a series of star appearances including Laurel & Hardy making a farewell tour of Britain. They needed the

[87] G-B. 1955
[88] G-B. 1948: Dan Birt

publicity and filled the place to capacity. Oliver was dying, and both comedians strapped for cash. They appeared, after a supporting bill, in a scene from the famous two-reeler *County Hospital,*[89] where Oliver lay abed during the sequence. He died a year later. Laurel, or Stanley Jefferson, was kept in comfort until his death many years later by Jerry Lewis, who based his act on Laurel.

Despite starring in countless films of the 30s, Leslie Henson made a pathetic figure, with few people remembering him, though his son Nicky has made a successful acting career.

Peter Sellers, as yet not internationally known, appeared in a one-man show entitled *A Goon.* He became morose and ill-at-ease for each photo shoot.

"Do I have to drink this coloured brown piss passed off as coffee?" he asked in front of Miss Adams, the owner of the Wedgwood Café, as, dressed as a waitress, she posed with him. She winced at me for bringing him to the Abington Street venue.

A few weeks later, the Lyon family opened a new furnishing store. Well-known at the time, due to the successful TV. series *Life With the Lyons,* Ben appeared with his daughter Barbara and adopted son Richard. Apparently Bebe Daniels was ill through over-work. Ben was an executive for Fox, and needed no television work. During a break for lunch, as they ate sandwiches while signing a pile of autograph books, I asked him about *Hell's Angels.* After convincing him I was not a journalist, finally he answered a few questions.

"No. I did not discover Jean Harlow. I'll tell you why I'm not keen to talk about *Hell's Angels.* We filmed it twice, once as a silent and again a year later. We really took off in those ancient flying coffins. Hughes wanted realism, and certainly achieved it! Sixteen men were killed making the film. Don't print this, please!"

Asked if they planned to produce another television series, he said "Not if I can help it. Bebe's made herself ill script-writing. She and Bob Block work twelve hours daily including weekends." It was strange meeting famous people, and seeing Ben Lyon face-to-face without scratch marks and change-over dots obscuring him!

After a few months I became advertisement manager for the 'Northampton Independent' with the press group. Pay was poor, and although I enjoyed the work, the prospects were not good.

The editor Bernard Holloway was, and remains in my recollection as, the most brilliant man I have ever met. He left the *Daily Telegraph*

---

[89] Hal Roach 1932: Charlie Chase

in the early 30s to take over the editorial chair of the '*Northampton Independent*', which his father had founded in 1905. Three of us put the flat-bed printed paper to bed every Thursday night – myself on ads., and Miss Gertrude Knight and Bernard editorially.

He and Lady (Joan) Wake for some years were engaged in saving Delapré Abbey. On one occasion her Ladyship entered excitedly.

"We must win, Bernard – must!"

"We shall be heard in loud voice. Pray be seated."

As she did so the wooden chair collapsed, amid her screams. Unperturbed, Bernard made no effort to help, looked down upon her trying to regain her feet, and held his cigarette pointedly to the ceiling.

"Ah, m'lady, what passes for office furniture here is deplorable. Northover! Do fetch Miss Knight. Perhaps a cup of tea for Lady Wake!"

Bernard was well-respected throughout town and county. He trained many journalists and ad. men. His publicity for the Repertory Theatre produced dividends, and Lou Warwick dedicated a volume of his Northampton Theatre History series to him posthumously (*Drama That Smelled*, 1975).

* * * * *

One by one, the public exhibitions ceased: only the monthly show for the Rushden Sanatorium remained. For this, I booked first-class products from the G-B. library at four pounds monthly, plus postage both ways. The six pounds fee covered costs and the projector in use. Since my early teens most of my evenings had been spent with films. It was odd having free evenings, and I felt lost.

The Essoldo cinema group, originally from the North-East, acquired the Regal, and immediately closed the place for an expensive refurbishment. They re-opened it, named Essoldo, on March 13th 1956 with *Cockleshell Heroes*, inviting the Mayor, the press, and members of the Royal Navy to attend both the première and, afterwards, a buffet and drinks party at the Wedgwood Café.

Lois and I quickly left the show to walk down to Abington Street as soon as I noticed the tabs marker on the final reel, to avoid the crowd. We arrived to discover the owner Miss Adams in waitress uniform flitting around the first-floor restaurant ensuring the cocktail niceties were all correct. A Chief Petty Officer who had been detailed to guard the drink was swaying about and offered: "Anything you want, my dears—Shush! Thish punch is good, or try a brandy. Shush! 'Ere they are!"

A group of people arrived, including Essoldo's managing director, Solly Sheckman, who was accompanied by the cinema's manager and an excited 'yes-man', who cried "I'm wearing my lucky shoes, Sir! Every new opening of all our many acquisitions, I wear these shoes, Sir. Another successful opening!" Joining them, I introduced Miss Adams as the m.d. ignored this twitterer standing on one leg and waving his other foot in mid-air. "You own this place, m'dear, and wait on tables. Tut-tut! M'dear lady – you must delegate - how would it be if I ushered patrons to their seats?"

An embarrassed Miss Adams muttered about 'preferring the personal touch' as quickly I joined Bernard Holloway (the Proprietor/Editor of the *Northampton Independent*: my employer) and his wife, representing the press. The place was rapidly filling with people including a naval officer and several sailors.

"No need to stay too long, Northover; just a drink to show the flag. I'm not keen on visiting cinemas – the play's the thing, you know!" He lit a cigarette, holding it at arm's length and pointing it to the ceiling, the other hand upon his hip; an attitude often copied by wags in the office. As I introduced Lois to his wife I noticed the C.P.O. swaying about with a bottle of rum in one hand and glass in the other. His officer, a good-looking man, had several attractive ladies surrounding him. Soft background music was scarcely audible over some sixty voices. Someone applauded as the Mayor and Mayoress arrived; apparently their car had been delayed in traffic. The Mayoress left her husband to join some ladies on the other side of the room.

My associate, Russell Harris, was drinking rum. His wife joined us with a *Chronicle & Echo* reporter. "Russ has been to the pub earlier. I hope he's not going to mix it up," she said, frowning in his direction. Russell merely raised a glass towards us, miming a toast. Suddenly the yes-man rapped a plate with a spoon to attract attention. "Ah! About time!" murmured Bernard, gazing at the ceiling. As the company quietened, the C.P.O. wandered across towards the Mayoress.

"Aha!" he cried loudly. "'Ere's the Mayoress." He placed an arm about the matronly figure as though she were a girl friend. Bernard sighed, "Northover. Go – rescue the Mayoress - at once!" As he spoke the C.P.O. quickly grabbed her chain of office and pulled the lady across the room as though she was a prize bullock at the County Show saying "How about this for a necklace, eh?"

I reached both of them as the C.P.O. laughed loudly, stopping in the middle of the room and glaring at me. "Whatcher want, eh? An' ain't she got a lovely pair of tits, eh?" Murmuring "Allow me, Your Worship," I tried to help her as the officer shouted "Chief! Get over here. At once." Her Worship smiled, eyes downcast, as the drunken C.P.O. lurched across to the officer. "Shur. Yes shur!" he blurted out as the officer commanded, "Get out of here at once!" Russell Harris strode over to join the C.P.O. "Now see here! So he's had a few. When I was in the Navy..." "You're not in the Service now. Get out, Chief!" With dialogue straight out of a Laurel & Hardy script, Russell said, "If he's going, then all right we'll stay as long as you like – er – er – then I'm going with him – right?"

Together they staggered from the hushed room. Within seconds a rumbling of stamping feet was heard, indicating they had fallen down the stairway. A deadly silence followed, broken by the Chief saying, "The buggers!"

At this, Bernard, who had remained hand-on-hip, gazing at the ceiling, remarked, "Those men are drunk!"

Locally, the cinema trade was terrible. I met Bob Munn down town. He had left the Gaumont for the Temperance Hall cinema.[90] Situated just off the Market Square, this show was undeservedly termed 'a flea-pit', and known to the older members of the public as 'Andrew's'. Difficult indeed to describe, the 'Temp.' was built on the corner of Newland and Greyfriars Street; no canopy, just a dark doorway with double stairs leading up to the show.

The projection box was a positive death-trap, with entry via an iron ladder fixed against the wall. Inside the hall, the box stood out from the back wall, and appeared as an after-thought. Surely the smallest projection room in Britain! Inside were twin Kamm machines with Kamm arcs and sound system. These were housed in metal streamlined blimps with only a few inches between them. The outside cowlings were removed for accommodating these massive machines. A tiny rewinding room adjoined on the same level. This small box overlooked the circle, and although the place had the shortest throw in town, the screen was the largest before other cinemas introduced wide-screen.

Film fare, unaltered for decades, consisted of six-reeler features, gangsters or westerns, plus a serial. A great number of Warner's

[90] Demolished. The site is part of the Grosvenor shopping centre.

second features were shown here to extremely good business. A first-run feature never appeared here to my recollection. Profits proved very high, yet spoiled by the fact that too many partners were involved. As late as 1956 the cheapest seats were still only 9d!

In the golden days of the thirties and forties, the public unable to find seats elsewhere on Bank Holiday Mondays and Saturday nights, flocked to the 'Temp.' as a last resort. Incorporated in the building were two religious assembly rooms and a dancing school. Beneath the cinema, a vast basement was rented to Mr. Smith for his sign-writing business. He laboured on for small returns until his retirement. His sons were firm friends of mine.

Bob showed me the box, certainly cramped in all respects; no-one six feet in height could stand upright; there was no air inlet whatsoever, so it was extremely hot and stuffy. "This place is on its last legs. Just running to the seats," he said. It closed in 1963.

* * * * *

At the newspaper more visiting stars were publicised in the daily broadsheet visiting shops and garages, while I worked away with the weekly *Independent*. We featured Errol Flynn as a news item. He was fat-faced, red-complexioned with a bloated look, and drinking hard. Being reminded of his eighteen-month stay at the Rep. did not interest him. At the time a scandal was hushed up, when he departed after a steamy affair with the producer's wife. A year after this visit he died, aged fifty-two.

My opposite number from the *Northants. Evening Telegraph*, Ray Wells, offered me double pay to move to the Kettering office of the East Midlands Allied Press (Emap). When Lois became pregnant in 1955, the hairdressing shop was sold and we purchased a house near Abington Park. After almost five years on local newspapers we sold the house and moved to Kettering.

Apart from attending local Chamber of Trade dinners, the evenings bored me. At 7.30 I would fidget, being unable to concentrate on reading, and finding television a complete bore. I found it difficult to believe that the third-rate programmes televised were preferred to an evening at the cinema. Independent TV. began, offering nothing to compare with the live theatre or the movies.

We made friends with an elderly couple next door, their two adult children, and some neighbours living opposite; and I operated a monthly show once more. Our lounge, two rooms with a dividing door, provided a suitably cinematic atmosphere. After the television fare, seeing the latest films in colour was much appreciated.

Ray Wells left the tabloid evening paper to introduce *Garden News*, and I became assistant advertising manager.

R. P. Winfrey, the managing director of 'Emap,' was showing some friends around the press room, handing them a copy of *Motor-Cycle News*, when suddenly he stopped the press. Opening the paper, a model dressed in a bikini costume sat astride a motor-cycle. Declaring this pornographic, he insisted over ten thousand copies were to be shredded, and the offending page re-cast. A wag described the barrister newsman as being so narrow-minded 'his head consisted of a double-sided ear.'

Finding the pressure of advertising a great strain, I decided to enter the fish-frying trade. Each day, the classified department girls would scan copy for any local fish-and-chip shops being advertised.

* * * * *

On occasional weekends, John Lawman visited us and stayed overnight on Saturdays. He was years my junior, and a very keen amateur photographer who made excellent pictures of our two young daughters, and had taken my place when I left the *Independent.* An accountant's clerk, poorly paid, and always short of money, he showed me a sleazy contact book. A small advert. sought nude photos for five pounds a set. He thought an innocuous series of pin-up photos of a recent girl-friend might sell, and I wrote a short covering letter enclosing the negatives to the box number. I gave John my roll of cut-out frames from the late-night de Luxe show of years before, and he asked if I would repair a 16mm. short.

Suspicious regarding the owner of this reel, he assured me one of his local associates wanted it repaired for a friend. It was in a dreadful state, with a splice every few inches, and torn sprocket-holes. A porno film, the projector managed to plough its way through it. Badly developed (the effect being soot-and-whitewash), blurred and full of jump cuts, it appeared to have been filmed in the twenties, entitled *We Girls*.

Within a month eight more reels of porno arrived for repair. These were easily serviced, and I finally persuaded John to name the owner. "Ordinary folk can't afford this type of film. One single reel sells for at least five hundred pounds," I told him. Quite unbelievable! A well-known manufacturer, whose national advertising embraced bill-boards, cinema, television, and the press. A Gaumont rep. had mentioned these 'stag-night specials' to me years previously, and their worth. Spliced together on one reel, I invited some friends from the newspaper to see a ninety-minute show. Two films featured Joan Crawford before she became a star.

I warned John that the condition of *We Girls* was such that further repairs were impossible. It was brought back twice in as many weeks!

Things were busy in the ad. department. Apart from forty calls weekly, plus features such as 'The Spring Bride', 'Carpet Fortnight', and various pubs enjoying a face-lift, a film star was due to appear locally.

After three years at Emap, I discovered the reason I had been poached from Northampton with double pay. They were under the impression that the film star shopping tours had been my idea. I decided not to admit that these lucrative features were instigated by Russell Harris of the *Chronicle*. The ad. manager explained – "Joan Rice is at the Savoy all next week in Arthur Miller's *A View From the Bridge*.[91] So I shall leave things up to you!" The first time this has happened since you joined the staff."

Meanwhile, at Rushden Sanatorium, the monthly shows declined in patronage. Saturday performances were transferred to a small ward, where barely a dozen up-patients attended. I wondered how long before the committee axe might fall. Over the years, medical science had almost eradicated Tuberculosis, and rumours were rife that the place might close.

This would surely finish my mobile career for ever.

* * * * * * *

[91] Like the Rex, Cambridge which Leslie Halliwell managed for some years, Kettering's Savoy Theatre was situated in a back street of terrace houses. Purpose-built, this show resorted to stage productions, and Northampton Rep. visited with a touring play for a dismal two years in competition with television. They tried alternating stage productions with films before the cinema changed hands, and was twinned.

13: Gaining a negative image

On a Monday night, just after ten, we were thinking of a light supper and retiring, when suddenly I realised the following morning Joan Rice was expecting a tour of the local shops. Over thirty-six shops were easily sold on the idea to consume four tabloid pages. A two-hundred word article was sketched out relating to her career. Setting up captions would prove tiresome, so I decided to obtain her approval for this copy and hand it to the compositors early in the morning, thus avoiding overtime.

Rushing round to the theatre, the curtain was down and Miss Rice, with a large bouquet in her arms, was surrounded by members of the cast and several news reporters. It had been a long day and I wanted to get back home and relax.

"Advertising! Excuse me!"

"I don't care if you're Lord Beaverbrook. Wait your bloody turn," a short fat reporter from our paper became annoyed. All too late! I was beside the star and showing her my piece.

"Thank you. That's fine. I filmed *Crowded Day* in 54, not 55. Otherwise, it's great"

"I'll see you in the morning," I promised. Brushing past the irate type, "Didn't take long, did it?" I remarked, and quickly departed for home.

The tour next day was extremely hard work. Few advertisers had prepared any worthwhile copy. By 6.30 pm, with the pages completed ready for Wednesday's edition, I was thankful to be home with Mahler's Fourth symphony relaxing me. Eating a light snack I wished the B.T-H. was quietly running beside me again in a village hall, and television not invented. Constantly, my mind returned to the rewinding room of the old de Luxe overlooking the fish-and-chip shop. The owner merely prepared potatoes and cut up fish. No dead-lines! No board of directors! No ad. manager to please! No hundreds of bosses who thought their ad. space the most important item of the press!

Drawing pencil sketches came easily to me after years spent designing posters. Yet these lay-outs cost me a good deal of time. Frequently, I spent lunch break in the car preparing ads., and until midnight trying to finish half-written ideas to hand to the compositors early in the morning. Each advertisement required the typeface indicated to fit the space perfectly.

From the beginning, I found selling space was comparatively easy—calling back to obtain the copy difficult! Often the client required to see a printed proof, and usually wished to alter the heading or part of the wording. This cost time and money in type-setting, thus a better method was a pencil lay-out. One page containing six spaces of the annual 'Hair and Beauty week' cost hours of work. Since this feature ran into six pages and embraced shops in various towns, allowing for travelling time, there was never a minute to spare. Three weekly papers went to bed at different times, and deadlines were hard to meet. Added to these features were car lists and estate agents. Smoking over thirty cigarettes a day, skimping meals, and sleeping badly, I missed life on the leisurely *Independent*. Most of all the loss of road showing was terrible.

During the week I enjoyed the Miller play at the Savoy, and was disturbed to find that Joan Rice's rôle was a small one, not worthy of the over-blown tribute I had penned: 'Kettering is indeed fortunate to enjoy an actress of the calibre of Miss Rice....' Phrases such as 'powerful performance' and 'unmissable' did not help her supporting part. On the Saturday I received a short letter of thanks from the actress "If only I had a press agent like you, I might have made Hollywood – thank you!"

At Finedon I met Mrs. Watts, owner of a small cinema in the town, plus two more situated at Irthlingborough and Burton Latimer. Using tiny type we crammed her programmes into a tiny little corner box ad. front page each Tuesday. I learned things were terrible for all three cinemas.

"I've cut back on everything. No more monthly show cards, very few posters, and paying flat-rate prices for old films. Television has ruined the trade. Very soon I'll be out of business," she complained.

Arranging for her advert. to be published free-of-charge for months failed to help. One by one, the cinemas closed, and the tiny advert. headed 'What's On At Watts Cinemas' went into the melting-pot.

* * * * *

John Lawman found himself a regular girl-friend, and his weekend visit became spasmodic. He left me with a packet of miniature photographs featuring nude girls, arms outstretched, entering the sea.

"Keep them if you like, nothing really."

We gave up hearing from the box number, for a five pound note sent months previously to this contact book.

Work piled up at the *Telegraph*. The identical month the previous year gave us thirty-five special feature pages to exceed, and we more than matched the revenue, yet the commission was halved! Apparently the management were to offer me the ad. manager position for the *Lynn News*, expecting me to move house later in the summer. This did not appeal to us. Lois refused to leave her native area and friends, and I found the prospect of living in King's Lynn, this flat, uninteresting part of the country, terrible to contemplate.

"But your career would really take off. Next step: general manager, and the board," advised the management, advising me that another chance could never be possible in the group.

Three police officers called at the house on Saturday afternoon, to ask if I had written to the box number concerned, of which they held a photocopy. A case was pending at Tamworth against the advertiser. Moreover, they produced a search warrant. We went upstairs where I gave them a few pin-up books and the miniature photos kept on top of my wardrobe. Here they found my 16mm. films and, quickly taking them out of the cans, held them up to the light using magnifying lenses.

"Our wedding film; a christening film; another one; that's a holiday reel," I explained quickly.

"And this one?" asked a sergeant. I'd forgotten that this old reel of repaired film was there, and tried, all too late, to explain away the content.

"This, and these small photos, are all pornographic. We'll have to take them. Pubic hair is deemed porno, you know."

They prepared to leave and I asked what I was being charged with.

"Nothing at all, Sir. Just helping us with our enquiries. Of course you'll need to attend court to show a just cause why these items should not be destroyed."

"Simple. Destroy them!"

"Cannot be done. It's up to the court."

On the Monday the management suspended me from work, pending the court hearing. The general manager was distressed by the affair.

"Can you imagine what Mr. Winfrey will say? There's a board meeting this week. I shall do everything I can to save your position here! We'll play it down; just a few lines, of course."

The court hearing was a fiasco. The magistrate, asking why I was not in the dock, was advised by the clerk to retire and view the pictures and film. Seated at the press table was the reporter with whom I had had the upset at the Savoy. He scribbled furiously, smiling with an air of satisfaction as the chairman returned to deliver a lengthy tirade. Red-faced he spluttered-

"If only it were within my power to send you down for a prison term. I have never seen such filth." He ended by saying, "You'll pay the costs of this court, seven shillings and sixpence."

As I left the court, the police sergeant drew me aside.

"Who owns the film? Very expensive, this type of thing. Must be a rich man. Who is he?"

Dialogue which followed did not appear in a television comedy series until many years later.

"Look into my eyes. You know you know who owns the film," he ordered.

I stared at him.

"Big man. Rich man. Household name, I think," he prompted.

"I do not know what you think I know, which you know about the owner of this film. I only know that I do not know the owner, and as I say do not know what you think I know."

Gibberish!" he retorted, adding in an undertone, "We know! You've wrecked your career. This man who you know owes you quite a lot – eh?"

"You're delaying me from enjoying my morning coffee at Barlow's. I've paid the court costs – good day to you!" I turned and departed.

The evening edition of the paper splashed a bold type heading across half a page, above the television offerings for the night –

Kettering Man Charged With Over 100 Obscene Photos

* * * * * * *

14: Positively the Final reel

Emap sacked me, and gave me a cheque for a full year's pay. Within a week I had secured a situation as ad. manager for Kettering Tyres. Smith and Brook backed by Goodyear tyres were regular advertisers. Starting with small premises in town, they paid rent and tyre money at the end of ninety days, Goodyear paying all the space ads. With only a tyre-fitter's wages to pay weekly, they opened twelve depôts around the county, plus others as far distant as Derby. They were the first to offer free puncture repairs. In those days garages fought shy of repairing punctures, and this innovation attracted many customers.

After eight months, with car provided, and pay in excess of Emap's salary, I enjoyed arranging ads. in out-of-town newspapers. The business flourished with twenty depôts opening swiftly. The partners planned to go public and were likely to be taken over by a national concern. My future appeared uncertain, and when a Rushden fish-and-chip shop was advertised, I purchased the place for three thousand pounds freehold.

Lois' Uncle Len ran a busy fried-fish shop business at St. Neots and prepared to sell-up and buy a farm. Perhaps those days at the de Luxe firmly registered in my mind: the fish-fryer made more money than Pascoe in the days of house-full cinemas. Only one boss to please—myself!

The Rushden shop was taking a hundred pounds weekly, selling fish-and-chips at 1/4d per portion. I opened on 5 November 1964. When we arrived from Kettering our fourth child was barely five weeks old. The first year proved hard work – we never enjoyed an evening out or a holiday break, but profits were good, and I quickly planned a routine of work giving me Wednesdays and Sundays free.

Cinema shows at the hospital were given on Friday afternoons, so this prevented the shop from opening on Friday lunch-time. I ought to have cancelled the films, and concentrated on the business.

* * * * *

Once again I organised a monthly film performance for our friends which was most successful. One couple, who ran an outdoor beerhouse at Finedon, arrived late, so to ensure they watched the whole programme, we started late, often about midnight. Afterwards everyone discussed the feature in depth. We became a critical circle, talking until the early hours and rarely breaking-up before 3am. Lois made coffee and bacon sandwiches, while for months the cream of M.G.M.'s later releases were shown.

Some years later I told my assistant to tell me her life story the next night. Television was showing *Jaws*[92] from 8.30 until our closing time of 10pm. As most women, her story was quickly related: left school, fell in love, married, and gave birth to a child. Trade, as predicted, was terrible, yet I wanted to stick to our regular hours. A small boy purchased a bag of chips at nine, and half-an-hour later we sold one piece of fish!

To pass the time I related the story of my sacking from the Telegraph and mentioned the name of the man who owned the cine film. Many years had passed, and the people concerned were of little consequence.

At the time I 'phoned John after the police visit. They called on him, but found nothing as he took my advice and had removed any photographs which might have been deemed pornographic. His

---

[92] Universal 1975: Stephen Spielberg

contact in town was protected by the local C.I.D. The illustrious owner of the expensive film library was never named by anyone concerned, although the police knew his identity. Since no-one admitted knowing him, nothing could be proved.

My assistant listened intently to my account and interrupted quickly as I mentioned the 'household name'.

"I've met him – recently. He loaned my friend and her husband a large amount of cash for their business at Irthlingborough. He's in a terrible state, an alcoholic, you know. I'm certain if you'd have named him to the police he would have killed himself. He could never have faced the disgrace. How terrible! It's a small world and no mistake."

Eventually, I ran the final hospital picture show. Few patients left their wards and television sets. After twenty-one years the monthly shows ended at the hospital.

And that, for films, was that!

Finally retiring in 1990, I spent over twenty-seven years running the fish shop. The various happenings with near-by neighbours and customers were so interesting and amusing that I penned a manuscript book for the grandchildren to read, entitled *A Pennyworth of Peace* – punning on the old phrase 'a piece and a penn'orth'.

A regular customer in the fish shop, a committee member of the local rugby club, asked if my equipment was available. He appeared agitated, and most excitable when he learned everything was in working order.

"The man who does the racing films is down with the 'flu. Can you help out, please? We're supposed to race at nine o'clock. Any chance you could show the films after you close the shop?"

"I'm open till ten. Be 10.30 before I can get to your club."

"We'll pay you well," he promised.

"What exactly are racing films. What gauge – 16mm.?"

"Yes, 16. We can race at, say, 10.45. Short horse-racing films. Members make cash bets on the winner. Each film lasts about 4 minutes, and come in sealed cans so no-one knows the winner. Very popular crowd-puller!"

Leaving the frying range for cleaning the following morning I sorted out the old 301. Strange yet true, I found frying fish-and-chips similar to projection. The pans are sieved after each fish load, and chips fried to clean the oil; similar in effect to potatoes cleansing the land after harvesting a different crop. Since one was constantly cleaning pans while switching off or adjusting controls, the practice seemed similar to cinema work. Returning to the lounge after the noisy hissing and crackling plus the loud crunching of the chipping machine, the effect of a television amid silent onlookers reminded me of entering the cinema. Very similar. I knew a fryer who considered charging his pans with the product like firing a steam engine. He was an ex-railwayman.

Carol Mizon, the author, Lois (his wife) and Marion Pannell

As I drove to the club the prospect of cleaning the range in the morning did not appeal: fairly easy when warm, a dreadful chore when cold. Outside the club the raucous shouting and laughing was reminiscent of the childrens' party at the working-men's club of yesteryear. In fact the atmosphere and many willing hands which grabbed the speaker and transformer proved a problem. As I swayed about on a ladder erecting the screen the projector moved like-wise standing upon a table.

One club member approached me looking furtively right and left before speaking. His attitude was that of an Egyptian street vendor about to ask 'You buy dirty pictures?'

"Look here," he muttered in a hoarse croak, "You want to make some money on the side? 'Course you do. Which horse wins?"

I assured him I had no idea. He gave me a look of disbelief as thankfully my customer rescued me. He frowned at the other man and held a tin aloft.

"Quiet. Quiet!" he screamed. As a fraction of the hubbub faded away he shouted once more. "Top secret. No-one knows the winner. See! Sealed box." He removed the sticky tape and handed me the reel. "Put it on your projector. There are six runners. Here's a list of the names and prices. Old Tom's ready to take bets. Give us a couple of minutes, Arthur, then off we go for the first film.

"How many films are there?" I ventured. He reached down to a small holdall. "Just four. O.K.?"

As the other man produced a leery disbelieving smile I threaded-up the film. A great commotion as the names were announced and a queue formed with hands stretched out with money. Eventually most of the lighting was switched off and I opened up the projector. Many splices clattered through, and I watched the machine closely, twice regaining a lost loop. Suddenly the sound failed. The exciter lamp had failed. This produced a groan from the packed club.

Turning off the motor I quickly selected a fresh lamp. Trouble! As I pushed it into the fitting the connecting locating strip gave way, and the new lamp was impossible to retrieve. This upset caused another great commotion. There was nothing but to restore the hall lighting, strip the projector casing, and remove the amplifier. As I struggled on, I asked if it mattered to run on silent.

"Oh, yes! It's the commentary. Very, very important. All O.K. now?"

Assuring my customer all was well, the show continued. During the final reel a splice split resulting in another total shutdown.

As I thankfully packed the equipment, one or two people made a collection of remarks – "Good job you've never run a cinema, mate!" "Never mind, it's only a toy projector." "Arthur, it's a good job you fry fish-and-chips rather than try to show films!"

* * * * *

Lauren, the eldest of our thirteen grandchildren, and home from university, impatiently awaits her cousin Nicola, some years her junior. The television which my wife rarely switches off is ignored as Lauren talks to Lois.

"We'll be late for the Kettering Odeon, Grandma. Titanic!"

"The fourth or fifth re-make," I remark. "Overlong by an hour to make room for a love story! *A Night to Remember* [93] is a better production, according to the critics."

"Critics," Lois exclaimed swiftly. "Take no notice of Grandpa who forever lives in the past!"

Nicola arrived out of breath and bubbling apologies.

"Do be careful when you come out. So many odd people around these days, and you'll not get home until ten thirty," Lois warned, adding "We'll watch the telly."

"The telly!" I decide to air my opinion. "The worst invention of the twentieth century! Approximately sixty-five million live in the U.K. Every night over forty million watch the box. Surely that's the reason why streets are deserted and dangerous from early evening? It begat video, which begat a Frankenstein's monster—the Internet!" Both girls laugh.

"We know why you dislike television, Grandpa," says Nicola.

"Yes," rejoined Lauren. "Years ago it ruined your mobile cinema. Did you really sit behind Grandpa on a motor-cycle, Grandma?"

"Oh, yes!" nodded Lois, "Wrapped in two overcoats, scarves, leather helmet, gum boots, and thick trousers with leggings."

"Oh, yes! The good old days," I sighed.

"Come along, Nick, let's go, and don't forget, Grandpa, today's life will be the good old days ten years hence."

They swiftly kissed my forehead and left as Nicola said, "Don't forget to lock the front door after us."

* * * * *

Occasionally I came across advertisers and compositors, from the *Telegraph* days—all asking the same question "Have you any pictures?"

In a Northampton café I noticed two ladies studying me and whispering to each other. Finally one approached me.

"Sorry to appear so rude, but my friend and I know you. It's just that we can't remember from where." Her friend joined us.

"I know who he is," she exclaimed, ""It's the Picture Man! You used to give film shows at Hanslope."

Both were in their fifties and grandmothers. I felt extremely old. The mobile cinema days were a lifetime ago.

In the small bedroom, a cupboard contains a variety of projectors,

---

[93] British 1956

cameras, and films. The B.T-H. 301 with stand and large spools is useless, as the leads from the projector to the transformer have perished with long disuse. Cine films, long since transferred to video-tape, are viewed with amusement by the family occasionally. They laugh at the out-dated ladies' fashions and the old cars – especially our wedding and the subsequent christenings.

In the transfer to video they have lost clear definition, but no projector remains to show them in fine clarity. In any event, no-one is interested in trying to set up any equipment for a show: simpler by far to press a button on the video-recorder.

* * * * *

Lois over-looks my writing pad:

"Do you really think anyone will be interested in reading about old cinemas or the mobile? I doubt it, and I'm convinced no-one will read a word!"

"Hmm. *The Picture Man*. Don't bother to deny it - you always were more in love with cinemas than me!!"

* * * * * * *

The Cinemas of Northampton: Equipment and Projectionists

Castle Cinema / St. James' Electric Cinema / Roxy, West Bridge. Former Roller-skating rink. Opened as Castle pre-1912 by Messrs. F.W. Giddings & J. de Chastelain. Derelict after WW1 military occupation. Became the **St. James'**. The installation was Gaumont Chrono machines and arcs with British Acoustic sound. The corrugated iron box was so hot in the summer that the operators worked in bathing costumes, resorting to overcoats in the winter. The sparsely-furnished and draughty auditorium seated 1,000, who could hear the trains from the nearby Castle station! It adjoined the Dover Hall, where medicals for the services were held throughout WWII. Re-opened as the **Roxy** in 1949. The entire complex was part of the Dover company's premises, which made lasts for the boot and shoe trade. A corner property near West Bridge, the site is now a block of flats.

The **Cinema de Luxe** Campbell Street, Lower Mounts: Opened in 1914. An early manager was Frank McClintock, with Frank Esmond as his assistant. (Later Esmond was to become the Opera House manager 1924/5.) After WW1, at least, it was owned by the National Electric Cinemas Co. Ltd. Harold Pascoe became a director of this concern, and in 1921 moved to Northampton to manage it for them, later buying it in 1929.

The Northampton public considered the show first-class, presenting first-run features, as did the 'Drome. In the first half of the 30s it was second in size to the Exchange.

From the street led a long rectangular vestibule, with the ticket office on the right. Behind this an iron spiral staircase led up to the compact and neat box with a small rewinding room on the same level. Twin large Ernemann V projectors and Strong 'Utility' automatic arc-lamps were mounted on Western Electric universal bases. The first sound system was Western Electric Wide Range, later Mirrophonic. When Harold Aspinal was the Chief, everywhere was spotlessly clean, and the large black spoolboxes were polished to a mirror finish. To the right of the box was a small room with a window overlooking the box. This held the non-synch. – a twin-turntable record reproducer. The fire exit from the rewind room opened onto a small flat roof some four yards square, and from here one looked down into the preparation room of the neighbouring fish-and-chip shop. The box was completely sound-proof from the auditorium.

The hall was long and narrow without a circle, seating c.1,000. The seating, all in good condition, was in deep orange, matching the house tabs. The acoustics were excellent, producing crisp first-class sound. All the back row seats were doubles, or 'love seats'. It was the first Northampton cinema to introduce them, quickly copied by the Regal. In recent adverts for Warner Village multiplexes these were heralded as new and unique!

It was redecorated in 1950, and earlier Pascoe had bought the former **Theatre of Varieties**, **Rugby** and successfully converted it to the **Scala**. In August 1950 he bought the **Empire**, **Kettering** from Joseph Lee. At this time his offices were at 55 Abington Street, where they were managed by Harold Binding. The de Luxe closed in November 1956. The building was soon demolished; the site was derelict and used for parking for many years.

Coliseum, Kingsthorpe Hollow: Opened 2 August 1920. Managing director J. G. Covington with general manager Harold Arnold (same pair as at Vaudeville Cinema). It was advertised as having over 900 plush tip-up seats. By 1927 it was owned by W. Harris, and later by John Norfolk, with films booked by his wife Mabel. Like the Regal, his other show, it then had Kalee 7s and arcs, but with Gyrotone sound. Bought by Eric Wright in 1948 who re-named it the **New Coliseum** in 1951 when re-equipping with all B.T-H. kit. It closed on 11 November 1958 with Nat 'King' Cole in *St. Louis Blues*. In August 59 it was bought and converted to a builders' merchant, which it is still. The façade was removed in the early 90s, but the date cartouche and corner pediment were saved and set up on the site boundary.

County Electric Pavilion, Gold St. (north side, near the top) opened c. 1910

The **Exchange**, later **Gaumont**, finally **Odeon**, was the town's premier (and largest) cinema from opening in 1920 until the Savoy in 1936, and was a reconstruction of the Corn Exchange, which had become semi-derelict by 1914, and in that year the company sold out to Major W. Hughes for £5,000, and went into voluntary liquidation. The proposal to convert the place "on a palatial scale both in size and splendour" was reported in the '*Northampton Independent*' in 1919.

It opened as a 1,916-seat cinema on Monday 2 August 1920 with *King Solomon's Mines* and *The Indestructible Wife* (featuring Alice Brady) from Mon-Wed, and *The Transgressor* and *Red Head* for the second part of the week. There was an orchestra of sixteen (within a week completed to eighteen), and though the Grand Concert Organ was incomplete, the player could add effects to the orchestral playing. Prices were Stalls 1/-, Balcony stalls 2/-, Balcony Fauteuils 3/-. (The 'straight' concert organ was later replaced by a cinema organ.)

Incorporated into it was a large restaurant and grill room, and above was a roof garden. It boasted its own bakery, which produced bread, cake and pastries. Tea was served to patrons in their seats during matinées. It was owned by a company of local businessmen, who sold it to Provincial Cinematograph Theatres (P.C.T.) in 1928, and thus became part of the Gaumont circuit when that company bought P.C.T., but for many years the luxurious carpeting carried the PCT monogram. Frank Slater played the WurliTzer[94] here for many years until the mid-30s, when he left to go to the Union Cinemas' Ritz in Hereford to play the Compton there. As later at the Savoy, all front circle seats were bookable. As a schoolboy, the author visited weekly, when the Jack Hulbert/Cicely Courteneidge features, Jessie Matthews musicals, and Will Hay comedies were shown here to full houses; plus the Astaire / Rogers musicals, until the Savoy screened the R. K. O. first runs.

Norma Talmadge appeared live on stage in October 1922 for the week in which her film *Smiling Thru'* was playing on the screen. Pre-talkies, in October 1925 *The Prince and the Maid* was screened as 'the first musical comedy picture'. The orchestra played the show's score, and there was a quartet of singers backstage. Real talkies came from 12 August 1929 when Al Jolson's *The Singing Fool* on sound-on-disc was shown. I remember attending a sound trailer in 1930 for *The Little Drummer Boy*, which amazed a chattering 'silent' audience.

Equipment after sound included Gaumont Eclipse heads and British Acoustic sound, and huge Hall & Connolly arcs with rotating positive carbon. These were replaced by Gaumont Kalee 21s after the war. For many years the Chief was 'Old Moley' (?real name Mould). The 21s were last operated by Bob Munn and his daughter Lesley, until the place closed in 1967 with a minimum of publicity.

---

[94] This was a 2-manual 8-rank instrument, which was transferred to the Picture House, Leicester. It is now preserved by Michael St. John Candy. *(Information from Jack de Coninck)*

Kingsthorpe Electric Cinema / Gem. Opened in October 1912 in the Liberty Hall, Washington St. There had been earlier pictures shown here, as early as 1898, but on a temporary basis. In 1928 the proprietor and resident manager was C. Goff, who booked the films at the hall. There were two programmes a week, and the films were run continuously. Prices then were 3d to 1/-.

The **Lings Forum Cinema** is part of the sports facility at Weston Favell shopping centre operated by the town council. This small show opened in 1976 using 16mm. equipment. The chief, John Ferrio, a personal friend, now has 35mm. and 16mm. in regular use. He was co-chief, with Ken Worley, at the Savoy/ABC/Cannon for twenty years until its closure. Ken became chief of the Virgin (now UCG) nine-screen multiplex at Six Fields, retiring in January 2002. They are two seasoned excellent projectionists, from arcs to tower projection, and both could handle cine-variety.

This view of the box shows a favourite lamp-house of the 30s, the Peerless Magn-arc, though now converted to zenon arc lamp rather than carbons.

Originally the **Studio**, the 200-seat Forum specialises in art, foreign, and second-run releases. Occasionally first-run features are screened. Prices are about two pounds lower than multiplex. A superb brochure is published bi-monthly. There is a noticeable lack of advertising for this cinema in the county. Few people in Rushden, Corby, or Wellingborough are aware of it.

Majestic 83, Gold Street on the Horseshoe St. corner. Opened in 1902 as the **Palace of Varieties**, with Fred. H. Anderson as proprietor, and Mr. Kemble as manager. There were 778 seats.

The opening of the New Theatre in 1912 caused conversion to films as **The Picture House**. This opened on Boxing Day, 1912, but failed. It was taken over by Leon Vint in September 1913, who was building a small Midlands/Wales circuit (about 15 houses). He renamed it **Vint's Palace**, and introduced cine-variety to the town. The box, situated under the circle, possessed the major draw-back that any patron entering or leaving the back row passed in front of the projection ports, thus obliterating the beam.

Illustration from the Sam Winfield Collection.

By 1927 the proprietor & manager was H. G. Hadland, from whom A.B.C. acquired it on 2 March 1931, to gain a foothold in the town.

They closed it on 26 June 1937, a year after opening the Savoy. It had B.T-H. projectors, arcs and sound system. Part of the site is the widened Horseshoe Street, and the rest is now Bell's corner.

New Theatre, Abington Street. Opened in 1912, it became the town's first cinema to use rear projection in 1933, using Kalee 7s and British Acoustic sound. First-run films exhibited were *House of Terror,*[95] *I Cover the Waterfront,*[96] and *The Private Lives of Henry VIII.*[97] The writer at the age of nine and ten enjoyed these three, and many more, before the place returned to variety in early 1935. Apart from films this author enjoyed the Lunts, many ballets, and symphony concerts there. In 1943 Constant Lambert conducted the London Philharmonic, who only just managed to squeeze themselves on stage.

In 1955 F. J. Butterworth offered this fine theatre to Northampton council for £10,000, but they refused, and the place closed in 1958 with *Strip! Strip! Hooray!* Nude shows attracted barely(!) sixty patrons per performance, although Laurel & Hardy on their farewell tour in 1954 filled the place for six days. My friend the late Lou Warwick, newspaper columnist and editor of the *Northampton Independent*, wrote and published the excellent book *Death of A Theatre*, available from libraries.

The **Picturedrome** (a.k.a. 'Robinson's') East Park Parade, Kettering Road: Opened 21 November 1912 as the **East Park Picturedrome**, on the site of a stonemason's yard. It was enlarged in 1919, and went over to talkies in 1930. Sold by Robinson to Harold Deighton Pascoe in 1935, who equipped it with Ross front-shutter projectors and Ernemann hand-fed arcs with Western Electric Wide Range sound (later upgraded to Mirrophonic). George Willis was the Chief here for over 21 years. He worked at the Savoy as Second for a few months in 1941 - leaving due to tunnel vision eyesight. He suffered twice from arc blindness.

During the silent days, where the Exchange possessed an orchestra, the 'Drome housed a quartet of musicians upon a small balcony to the left of the screen. In the thirties, prior to the opening of the Savoy, first-run Paramount and M.G.M. films were shown here. This cinema shared Paramount News with Pascoe's other acquisition, the Cinema de Luxe: the only shows in town to use this superb newsreel.

---

[95] Universal 1933
[96] Twentieth Century 1933: James Cruze
[97] London Films 1933: Alexander Korda

Incidentally, the Gaumont News was not shown at the Gaumont Exchange, which used Fox's Movietone. G-B. News ran at the Ritz, Tivoli and Plaza, and a ten-day old edition ran for some years at the 'Temp.'. The Coliseum used Universal, which opened with a silhouette of a male commentator with the voice-over "Here is the Universal News: the golden voice of the silver screen." It was very nasal on a poor sound system.

Publicity stunt and queues in 1928. *Illustration from the Sam Winfield Collection.*

It was the first independent cinema to install wide screen, though without financial success. Pascoe had to close down in December 1958 due to the impact of television, and in June 1959 he was reported to want between £6,000 and £7,000 for the building.

After a spell of closure, it re-opened as the Rutland bingo hall. This itself closed, and in the middle 90s the place re-opened as a café-bar, appropriately named The Picturedrome. How entertaining it could be if the present owners, the Richardson brothers, were to arrange an authentic 'silent films evening', with a film projected from the box, and a quartet of musicians playing from the original, still-existing, gallery.

Ken Osborne's interest in film started as a boy when he would cycle visiting the local cinemas. On leaving school he began training as a projectionist in the Picturedrome, and went on to work in a number of local cinemas including the **Wellingborough Lyric** and the Essoldo/Regal. In 2000 he celebrated 45 years of his local Mobile Movies film and video business, sold it and retired.

The Plaza, Wellingborough Road was originally known (and often referred to by older people) as 'Bentley's'. Opened in 1910 as **East End Picture Palace**, then **King's Picture Palace**, bought in February 1913 by a chain. They provided 'dainty teas' at Thursday matinées. Featured private boxes seating five. It ran under various names such as **Abington Park Cinema**, finally closing in the late 20s with variety acts as the **Prince of Wales' Playhouse**.

It re-opened as a cinema in 1932 with a documentary feature *Igloo.* Equipment was Gaumont Chrono machines (later replaced by Eclipse) and G-B. hand-fed arcs, with British Acoustic sound. Charles Lawson operated alone for years until the place closed in 1969. A black ceiling was surrounded by cream arrows a few feet from the walls. In front of the screen was a rock garden with shrubbery and a fountain, all built by Charlie. There was no circle, but a small balcony beside the box seated four people. In the latter 30s the entire staff, manager to doorman, except Charlie, was sacked for fiddling the tickets.

After opening the Ritz and the Tivoli, local businessmen Harris & Faulkner acquired the place. Later brothers Myer and Sydney Cipin bought all three. There was new equipment: Westar with Westrex sound and arcs was introduced with CinemaScope films. Charlie had a few years with modern equipment after using antiquated equipment for a quarter of a century!

In 1969 the Plaza closed, and Charlie was transferred to the ambiguously-named Regal-Plaza Bingo Club at the Grove Road cinema to show afternoon matinées for children during school holidays. Here, six months later on 19th December, he collapsed in the box thought to be eighty years plus. It was suggested he died of 'a broken heart'. One imagines he would have preferred his demise to have been in his beloved Plaza.

The **Ritz**, Welford Road, Kingsthorpe. This cinema opened in 1937, two years after the Tivoli, Far Cotton, by a friend's uncle W. Harris, a leather factor, in conjunction with F. Faulkner, a local seed and feed merchant. Fred Irons was the chief here, transferring from the Majestic. Both cinemas were equipped with Kalee 11s (Indomitables), Kalee auto arcs, and R.C.A. Photophone sound. Neither show boasted a circle. Doug Woodford returned from war service in the R.E.M.E. to become Chief of the Tivoli. These shows, including the Plaza, gave their owners some clout in booking from the renters. Known as H. & F. Cinemas, both were sold in 1949 to the brothers Sydney and Myer Cipin, whom the author knew for some years.

Sydney also owned the **Regal Daventry**, and worked extremely hard keeping the show open during massive modernisation in the 60s. Plans included special access for wheelchairs, and it is believed the work and worry hastened his early death. Myer appeared in *Boys Will Be Boys*, an early Will Hay vehicle.[98]

The **Regal**, Grove Road, formerly the **Vaudeville**, was opened in March 1920 for variety, and later films. The two 'bioscope' machines were either made by, or simply supplied by, the firm of Bassett-Lowke, Ltd., best known for engineering models.

Re-designed in 1929-30, the lessee was John Norfolk, and whose wife arranged film bookings. Whereas the Ritz, Tivoli and Plaza were pleasantly but plainly decorated within, the Regal had six large Spanish scenes, painted by an unknown but excellent artist; three on each side, lit from underneath.

Various equipment was used in the cramped box, including Kalee 7s, Kalee arcs and Morrison sound, the B.T-H. machines, arcs and sound, and finally the Westar projectors, arcs and sound were transferred from the Plaza after closure there.

After becoming the **Essoldo** it closed finally in 1968. The building still stands, stripped internally.

Temperance Hall (a.k.a. as Andrew's) Newlands. It was opened as the town's first permanent cinema by A.H. and E.H. Andrews in September 1908. Before that it, like other local halls, had often had touring bioscope shows booked in. The Andrews brothers had become cinema exhibitors as early as 1902, and floated as a public company in 1910. The T.H. closed in 1963, when it was claimed to be one of the longest-running cinema ventures in the country.

Although the seats were cheaply priced, it enjoyed good business with second-run six-reelers and serials. The profit was poor by being shared by too many businessmen. No first-run film was ever exhibited in the days of sound. The equipment in my time was Kamm projectors, arcs, and sound, all being designed by Sydney Kamm. This cinema possessed the shortest throw from box to screen, and the largest screen in town before wide screens were introduced. The last projectionist to operate in the tiny, cramped box was Bob Munn.

Tivoli, St. Leonard's Road, Far Cotton. This was built on the site of a former coal yard, probably associated with the near-by canal arm. It

[98] G-B.1935: William Beaudine

was the last purpose-built pre-war cinema, being another venture of Messrs. Harris and Faulkner It opened in July 1935 with 832 seats on two levels stadium-style, with no circle. Sound was R.C.A. It ran continuous programmes with prices from 6d to 1/6d. At the end of the war Harris & Faulkner sold their Northampton cinemas interests to Midland Super Cinemas, and by 1948 prices had risen to 7d. to 1/9d.

On return from war-time army service Doug Woodford became Chief here. It closed in August 1960, and still stands, recognisable as a former cinema.

The **Savoy / ABC / Cannon**, Abington Square. Well-known local builders Glenn's constructed this lovely cinema throughout 1935, to the plans of architect William R. Glen*, F.R.I.A.S.* The author met Mrs. Glenn, Senior, and other members of the family at a public meeting in 1994, with a representative of M.G.M., the then owners, hoping to save the cinema from closure. Doug Woodford transferred from the Majestic at the 1936 opening to become third operator in a staff of five, Frank Heighton being the chief. Like Mrs. Glenn, Doug possessed a copy of the attractive opening souvenir brochure.

The site was a semi-triangle, and appeared like a rubbish tip skirted by tall wooden hoardings, plastered in an haphazard manner by tatty fly-posting. Thus when the white stucco front appeared bearing the letters S A V O Y above huge neon-strip-lit columns in May 1936, the effect on the public was electrifying. The main entrance on the corner of Lower Mounts and Abington Square was flanked on each side by three shops. Overhead, a semi-circular canopy contained the words *Broadway Melody of 1936*, the opening film.[99] On the steps leading to the vestibule twin signs proclaimed 'Wilfrid Southworth at the Compton Organ' on one side, and the other read 'It's Cooler Inside. Fully Air-Conditioned'. Within yards of passing the cinema building passers-by and patrons were aware of the hygienic aroma, a scent distinct to the Savoy, which pleasantly filled the place.

The spacious vestibule had two pay desks for stalls and circle. The 6d front stalls had their own entrance 20 yards along Lower Mounts, where frequent queues heard the hissing of the plenum chamber entrance above. Front stalls patrons did not sit lying back suffering aching necks as at the Exchange: the Compton organ console in the centre of the flower-decked orchestra pit meant there

[99] M.G.M. 1935/6: Roy del Ruth

was an 18 yard depth to the screen set back on the full-sized stage. Three pairs of tabs (curtains) were available—massive house tabs filling the proscenium with screen tabs behind for cinema, controlled from the box, and another pair could be used for live performances.

The sixpennies merged under the circle with the 1/- rear seats, totalling over 1200 on the ground floor. The front (2/-) and rear (1/6) circle patrons, separately divided, approached through a large, thickly-carpeted vestibule to enter the 630-seat balcony. Front circle seats were bookable. All seating was in staggered rows, ensuring a clear view of the screen with its straight corners: the only cinema in town not to have rounded corners. *Pathé Gazette* news was shown, also *Pathé Pictorial* and *The March of Time* every few weeks.

Seated in stalls or circle patrons were encircled by the massive ante-proscenium, with two arched lighting coves tastefully lit by ever-changing colours, outstanding during intervals and organ interludes. The entire cinema walls and ornate ceiling were in orange and yellow. All seating comprised identical chairs with padded arms, and each row was nicely carpeted.

A staff of twenty-five, including two page boys, was paraded daily at 1.45 in the circle foyer by the manager, excluding projectionists, for Frank Heighton would have none of this time-wasting.

The projection equipment has been described in earlier chapters. Several organists appeared here, and the best-known was Josef Flitcroft, whose son still plays. 'Flitty' adopted 'Alone', the hit song from *A Night At The Opera*[100], as his signature tune. Other musicians included Raymond Charles and Harold Nash.

(The latter was one of two pianists who played for several years at the **Northampton Repertory Theatre**. Opened as the **Royal Theatre & Opera House** in 1884, no films were shown here, and weekly repertory commenced in 1927. It adjoins the large Derngate entertainment centre, now presenting monthly productions, plus the inevitable Christmas pantomime.)

Until continuous performances commenced in 1938, there were three separate shows daily: 2.30, 5.45, and 8.30, with the cinema being vacuum-cleaned after each house. Worth a mention is the noisy, dusty, foul-smelling tiny room adjoining the downstairs vestibule, where the vacuum motor plant was housed, producing powerful suction for the cleaning staff. Pipes from here lead all over the theatre to hose points in the wall skirting boards, where air-tight

---

[100] M.G.M. 1935: Sam Wood

covers could be lifted for the hoses to plugged in. This meant all the dust went outside, not simply re-circulating as in domestic equipment.

During my work at the cinema eventually I sat in the rear circle back row for tea breaks. Frequently I heard a rustling sound—a piece of paper, a bag perhaps—being explored by a rat. Oh yes! Rats were a menace until the invention of Warfarin. One wondered exactly the effect upon patrons, ladies in particular, had they known of this infestation.

In 1941, Fred Allen became chief, the first film he projected being the war-time R.A.F. semi-documentary *Target for Tonight.*[101] He remained in charge until the Savoy, by then long ABC, was tripled in 1973/4. This coincided with his retirement. He lived only four streets away from my home, near Abington Park.

After much work and stress during live shows, the local operatic society rented the show for a week annually. Fred experienced many sound problems: although sound from a live show could be deafening for front stalls and circle, it was muffled and poor quality beneath the circle for the rear stalls.

With the popularity of television, three-dimensional films were shown, when the public were supplied with throw-away special coloured spectacles. This was a nightmare for projectionists—much worse than operating sound-on-disc films some thirty years previously. Both projectors ran a copy of the film simultaneously, which meant an interval after fifty minutes, as the 20-minute 2000' spool-boxes were replaced by 6000' ones. The Warner Brothers' re-make of their *The Mystery of the Wax Museum,*[102] entitled *The House of Wax*[103] was the first film shown using 3-D: a very poor imitation of the former. This incorporated chairs in a fight scene being hurled at a ducking audience. Thankfully for all concerned this expensive gimmick was short-lived, and abandoned by the industry. Warner's were obliged to put out the same film as a 'flat' booking—nothing to do with the money involved as a flat percentage cash booking, but a 'normal' film.

Fred was thankful to retire, and showed me the 'cake-stand' being installed for the twin cinemas under the circle, identical with that in the top box. Closed-circuit television gave operators in the top box a view of the two downstairs screens. "No tabs for these screens. Imagine it, eh?" Fred remarked, referring to the small cinemas.

---

[101] Crown Film Unit 1941: Harry Watts
[102] Warner Bros 1933: Michael Curtiz
[103] Warner Bros 1953: Andre de Toth

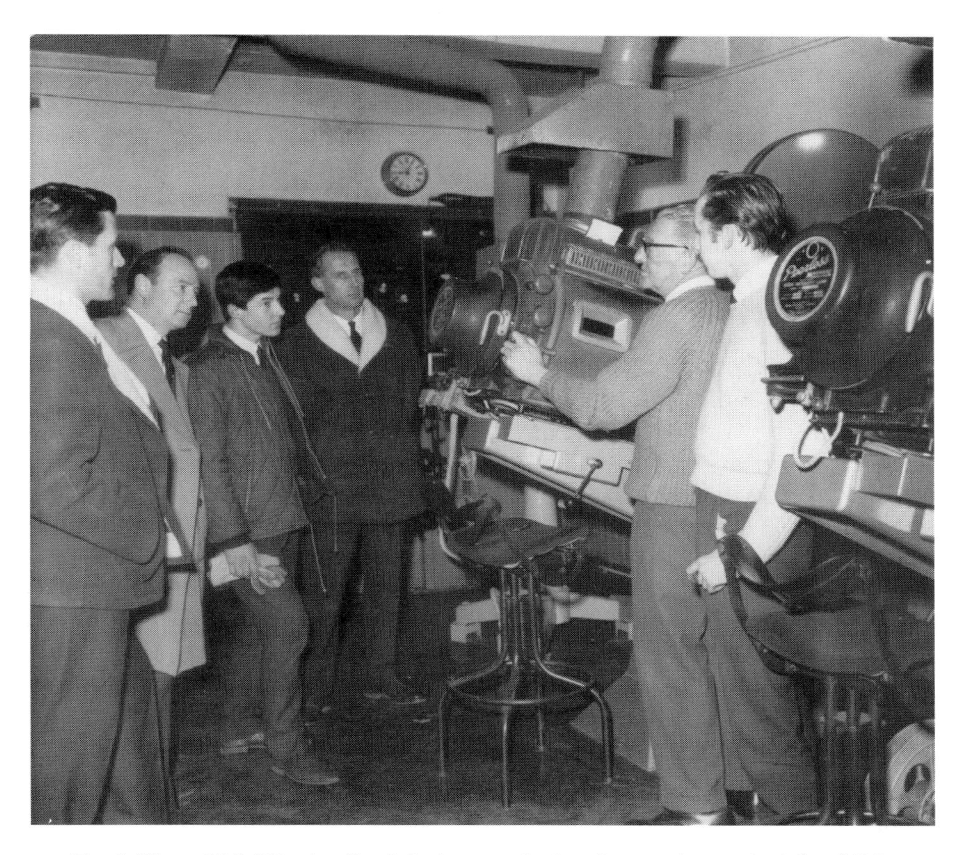

Fred Allen, Chief Projectionist, demonstrates the equipment at the ABC.
Photograph by courtesy of the Northampton Chronicle and Echo.

The magnificent circle remained, also, if required, the front stalls from stage to the circle on the ground floor. Where many decades previously the Exchange enjoyed a visit from the American conductor/composer John Phillips Sousa, Fred operated stage lighting and effects for the Beatles. Sadly, he died after a few months of retirement, as did his former Second of many years, George Baker, also within a year after retiring.

The Savoy, as the ABC, in the final week as a single-screen operation.

(Photograph by courtesy of the Northampton Chronicle and Echo.)

Murder on the Orient Express[104] was the first film shown from the top box (now ABC1) in 1974, after a short closure, during which time Northampton was without a cinema. The cinema rose phœnix-like from the ashes of financial loss caused by television and easy availability of hire-purchase. Over the years the attendance dwindled to an all-time low in 1984. Later, the Cannon circuit purchased the building, and finally MGM, who closed it when their new Sixfields 9-screen multiplex opened. This produced an outcry from regular picture-goers, who mourned the loss of their town centre cinema. An expensive 'bus ride was now required, or a long walk .

Originally the Savoy possessed a large car park for over 200 vehicles. Rushden entrepreneur David Hamblin, owning nearby

[104] GB/EMI 1974: Sydney Lumet

property, bought the car park, and let drivers park for 25p daily. Within a year or so the council bought the land for their multi-storey car park.

The Savoy / ABC / Cannon / M.G.M. closed in 1993. The author produced a short video prior to the closure, and met a representative from English Heritage and the important planning executive from M.G.M. Together we stood upon the stage as the Heritage people were apparently amazed to discover back-stage dressing rooms. "Hmm!" murmured the planning executive as we surveyed the auditorium. "Was it a disused old shoe factory once?"

My eyes were on the ports of the long projection suite at the rear. I had stared up at them as a child, annoying a young couple seated behind me and other patrons. "This kid in front keeps watching us," said the girl. "Sorry, I'm only watching the projection room."

I remembered Irene, my first girl friend, beside me on the circle back row, kissing and cuddling during my 30-minute supper break.

In the 80s the Compton organ from the Ritz, Cleethorpes was installed - here is the console on the lift, and one of the two pipe chambers being set up.

(Photographs by courtesy of the Northampton Chronicle and Echo.)

When I returned Chief instructed me to show the air raid lantern slide: I used the wrong slide..."No! Not an alert! The all-clear's been sounded!" cried Chief, adding "Where the hell have you been, boy?" Of course, he never met the lovely Irene.

These reminiscences flooded back as I gazed at the circle back row and the box above. All gone forever. I thought of the faces which stared out of those ports – Frank H., Doug W., Mrs. Wickes, Burgess, Bob B., Alan Ashton, Pringle, Fred A., George B., Ken W., and John F. while this ignorant fool continued, "The whole place will go rotten. Probably end up on fire!"

Thankfully, his prediction proved wrong. Finally, after a long fight with the council, the Jesus Fellowship has acquired the former cinema as an assembly hall with facilities for young people and a snack bar etc...also as a venue for the homeless and drug-addicts. They intend keeping the circle, stage, and screen to let out for amateur theatre use. So the Savoy is saved from being vandalised by a company who, approved by the council, wanted to destroy the circle and operate another night-club. The Exchange suffered a similar fate some years ago.

Envoi

The Plaza is a bank, the Ritz a chapel, the Tivoli a motor works. The Coliseum is a builder/plumber's merchants' store, the Roxy a block of flats, the Regal a defunct gym. The de Luxe is a patch of bare land, and the Majestic a store. The Temperance Hall was demolished when the Grosvenor Centre was built: Jones (Jeweller) and Nationwide above on the site. Only Pascoe's Picturedrome retains its former dignity in restoration.

Between 1949 and 1953, my mobile cinema operated in the following locations: Creaton, Spratton, Brixworth, Ashton, Roade, Hanslope, Hartwell, Walgrave, and Broughton. All the village halls are still in use with the exception of Silverstone, now a bank, and Harpole Band Institute, long since a house. Creaton Sanatorium is a housing estate, while Rushden Sanatorium is a normal hospital and medical centre.

For many Northamptonians, these buildings will recall hours of tinsel and make-believe, and evenings of cinematic pleasure. The Savoy – the last of the town's many cinemas from the golden age of the movies - is saved to be a restored picture palace.

* * * * * * *

Sydney (left) **and Myer** (right) **Cipin as owners of the Plaza, making a presentation in the foyer.** *(Photograph by the Northampton Chronicle & Echo.)*

1936 – A Year to Remember

So Mother visited California and I stayed at home from March to October! But what of the films in this particular year? Here are only a few outstanding productions I recall with pleasure. All are noted in my film diary, as I do not rely solely on Halliwell.

BROADWAY MELODY OF 1936 The Savoy Northampton opened with this. M.G.M. Roy de Ruth. Songs included 'You are My Lucky Star.'
THE GREAT ZIEGFELD M.G.M. Robert Z. Leonard. Also at the Savoy, running for 179 minutes thrice daily. With Ray Bolger (Scarecrow *in The Wizard of Oz*), and the famed Fanny Brice. Luise Rainer, who won the Academy award, followed this with M.G.M's *The Good Earth* in 1937. Sidney Franklin, the director, and she both won Academy awards. This, also a lengthy feature ran for 138 minutes.
A NIGHT AT THE OPERA M.G.M. Sam Wood. The first vehicle in which wonder boy of the studio, much-lamented Irving Thalberg, placed the Marx Brothers into a musical background.
SWING TIME R.K.O. George Stevens. Far better than *Top Hat*, this Astaire/Rogers hit had music by Jerome Kern, including 'A Fine Romance' with superb production values. As all the pair's musicals, choreography was by Hermes Pan.
NIGHT MAIL The famous 24-minute documentary by John Grierson. Music by Benjamin Britten and the outstanding poem by W.H. Auden - unmissable.

Today, I note nothing mentioned by critics worth paying £5.80 to see, and to have my eardrums suffering over-loud sound. As for the acting – really! *"Hugh Grant? Just a floppy young stammerer. Four Weddings and a Funeral - dull rubbish from British studios. All same-y, aren't they? Yet America laps them up."* Not my words, but Peter O'Toole in the *Sunday Mail* 14 April 2001. What picturegoer can possibly argue with such an observation? The foul-mouthed unfunny offering *The Full Monty* was a ten-reel bore. I was obliged to view both on videos hired by Lois. A 'hotted-up' version of Sherlock Holmes is apparently in production. Basil Rathbone was perfectly cast in *The Hound of the Baskervilles* in the 1940s, yet Hollywood brought the character up-to-date later capturing Nazi spies in six-reelers for Universal.

Why don't British studios film the life of discredited M.P. Horatio Bottomley, who conned money from people, and published 'John Bull', the 30s weekly. He ended in the gutter after appearing on stage at the Windmill. Again, can no director or company remake Sandy Wilson's *The Boy Friend*, which Ken Russell made a mess of in 1971 starring 'Twiggy', who was too inexperienced to take the leading lady rôle, though now she could carry it off.

If these statements read like the observations of an angry old man – they are! I make no apologies for them!

Supplement:

THE MAN IN THE BOX
(A BRIEF EXPLANATION OF CINEMA OPERATING)
Arthur E. Northover 1940

When you relax comfortably in your cinema seat and prepare for a good evening's entertainment, do you ever think of the men and women behind the scenes? The answer is yes, perhaps you do think of the stars, the technicians, camera and sound men. But there is one person forgotten and unheard of by practically everyone. The man in the box. The film operator, the man who is responsible for reproducing the film on the screen. He works in the projection room (commonly termed 'the box' by projectionists owing to its small confined space). From that room and that room alone your entertainment emerges in a ray of brilliant light, to be reflected to you via the silver screen.

Of course it is ridiculous to assume that all who visit the cinema should wonder what the projectionist is doing: that would only ruin a evening's enjoyment. But surely more knowledge should be gained about this almost forgotten man. That is what I hope to accomplish by this brief story of cinema operating. The facts of this story are true. I gained them by associating myself with cinemas, and the people connected with them. My period of cinema employment was brief, but in that time I gained a great deal of worth-while knowledge.

Let us review the projectionist's past life in a few paragraphs. Supposing we commence in 1920, the period when cinemas were getting well into their stride as a source of foremost entertainment the world over. It was at that time that technically minded youths were looking to the future. They knew then, long before sound films, that the silver screen would be the world's future entertainment.

So they grabbed their chances while they could, studied hard at electricity and other technical data. They commenced their world of the future by turning the handle – working in hot projection rooms turning the old hand-cranked machines for hours on end. The projection rooms were small, unhealthy, and hot; barely enough space for two men to occupy in comfort. Thus the word "box". That name for the projection room has stuck, and I doubt if it will ever be changed.

After working hard for several years, came the advent of sound. The shadows on the screen were really talking, the public crowded the box office, and the queues seemed everlasting outside the picture palaces of those days. But the man in the "box" was never heard of, never mentioned. Yet it was his skill and determination that kept the sound going, and the picture on the screen. More worries were added to his ever increasing list: the worry of perfect synchronization of both sound and film. The film had no sound track on, the sound being supplied by a record. Therefore when one started up the projector, the record had to be started at precisely the same second. And yet with all this extra responsibility he received no word of comment, and no part of the enormous profits being made by the film magnates. His wage was cut, his hours increased, in fact his life became a living hell.

Then in early 1931 came sound recorded on the film itself – more drastic changes, more scrapping of equipment, in fact more work and worry. All this was dished out to the film operator. Strikes ensued as a result and the film operator practically became headline news. However, this was short lived. Unemployment was so vast in the cinema industry that other operators soon replaced those on strike. Having to work for more hours for half the money was the result. No!, strikes did not improve matters, they merely kept wages down. In Liverpool about this time there was revealed a case where a cinema projectionist and his wife (who was a cinema cleaner in the morning and an usherette at the performances) were earning the absurd amount of fifty shillings a week *between them*. Astonishing but quite true.

Since then, operating as a career has certainly improved, but not a great deal. Wages are still low (£3-10–0 being the average wage of a chief operator) and many of the cinema “boxes” are still small and unhealthy, but I believe in the future, projectionists and all cinema workers will receive the recognition that they fully deserve. Today the ‘man in the box’ looks to the future, believing that soon television will probably replace the cinema as an entertainment source.

Chapter II – The Projection Room
(The Projectors, the arc lamps, and the explanation of sound)

In this chapter I intend to deal fully with the projection room and the equipment housed in it. The first-class box has in it all the latest equipment (or should do), therefore it is only natural that a more perfect performance by the projectionists should be given. So I will discuss the small cinema and its projectors first.

The small projection room – 800 seater 'Kalee 8' heads, with EMEL H.I. arcs and Western Electric Mirrophonic sound type LB 35 g/dtns/ac

The above illustration was taken of the Highbury Cinema, Bulwell. On the left is the "non-synch." – to you this technical expression means where the gramophone records are played. You will then observe the two projectors are termed as Number 1 and 2. This is an important factor in the running of the 'box'. First we will take the arc lamps and study them in detail. The projectors are composed of three main parts: 1. The Arc Lamp 2.The 'Head' 3. The Sound System. So let me take first the arc lamp in detail.

The Arc Lamp

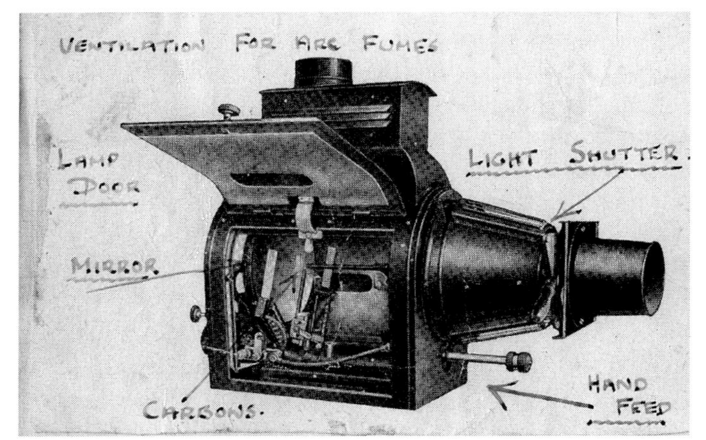

This is a photograph of a German "Zeiss Ikon" Artisol Arc Lamp, hand–fed, with magnetic control. The main points of the arc are, as you can see, the carbons, the clamps, and the mirror. The clamps merely hold the + and – carbons in position. The mirror is the means of reflecting the light of the carbons towards the screen.

The 'Hewittic' twin rectifier

Some small cinemas use low-intensity carbons which burn much more slower than H.I. The advantage with high intensity is the brilliant white light which produces a much clearer picture than the other.

The current for the carbons in a.c. arc lights comes either from the mains through a rectifier, or from a generating plant, via the arc resistances which are needed to cut down the feed to the required voltage.

The best type of rectifier for this work is the mercury arc. Considered as the best and the most popular is the Hewittic brand, used in all the leading cinemas and theatres in the country. These rectifiers are about ten feet in height, and in the large cinema are kept in a separate room away from the 'box'. To have them in the box is breaking the law. Some of the older cinemas, however, take this chance owing to limitations of space.

The rectifiers and the arc lamps must be kept scrupulously clean by the operator in charge. Of course, there are many types of arcs, and makes, which will appear in later chapters of this story.

The Projector Head

The projector mechanism, or 'head', as it is most commonly called, is the most important factor. The illustration on the left is the Ernemann VII B mechanism. This is a German production.

The film is fed from the top spool by the top steady-feed sprocket. Next it continues to the 'gate', which is a steel plate with a square-cut aperture, which just coincides with the picture frame on the film. The gate is where the beam of light from the arc lamp is directed, and from there it is magnified through the powerful lens to the screen. Running from the gate the film continues to the intermittent sprocket, which pulls the film one picture at a time through the gate, thus giving the picture movement.

As the film is pulled through the gate, a small shutter (concealed in this photograph), cuts off the arc light each time the picture is pulled through, thus eliminating all flicker on the screen. From the intermittent sprocket the film passes to another steady-film sprocket to be fed from there to the sound unit.

The thread-up of the Ernemann is rather difficult for the layman to follow, but between each sprocket is a loop in the film. These loops must be left for the required 'play', whilst the projector is in motion. The projector must be kept free from oil and grit, for if any grit was left in the gate, a film would be scratched after one showing. The machines are generally covered up when not in use, and oiled daily.

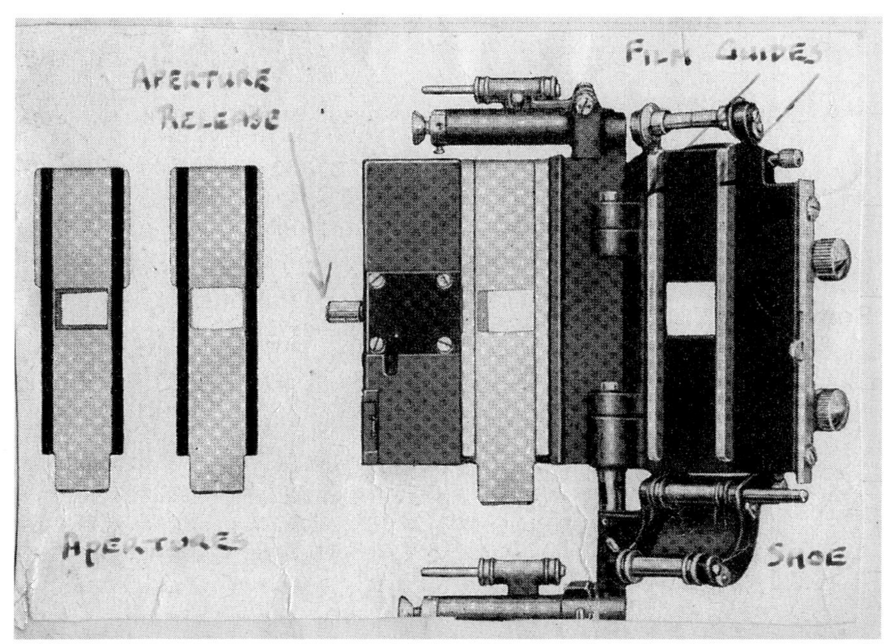

These are the most important points of the 'head', so next let us look at the sound system.

The sound system

Sound, a very important factor in the cinema, is not easily explained on paper. The system consists mainly of exciter lamp, lens tube, and photo-electric cell. I hope to convey to the reader some brief idea of its working by means of the diagrams. The sketch is of a sound-head.

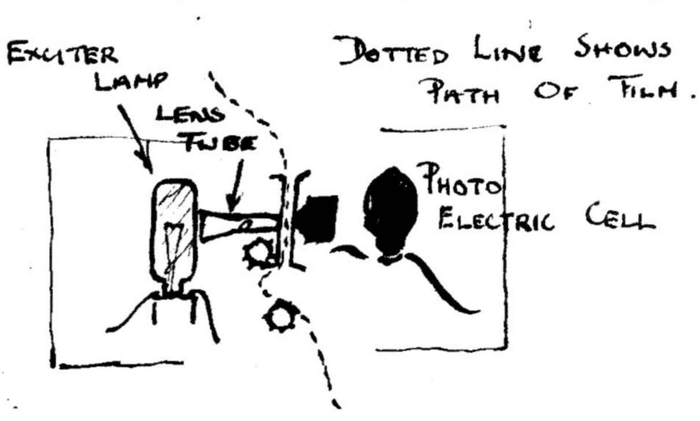

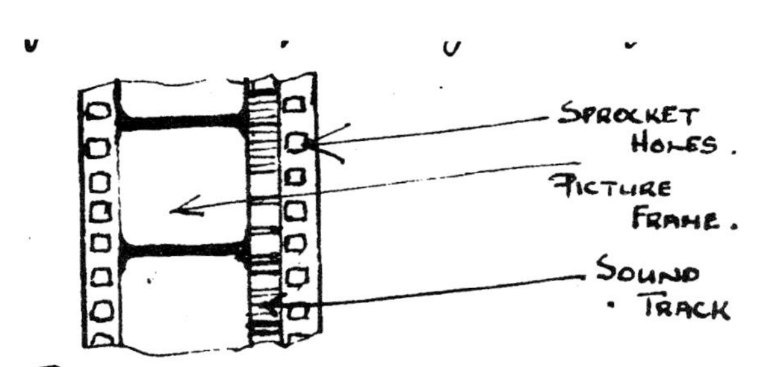

The sound track on this piece of film is composed of small black lines. These are the sound, just as the grooves are sound on a gramophone recording. The means of reproduction is the sound unit, which is just below the 'head'. The diagram shows the interior of the sound head. The small wobbly lines on the film sound track are really sound vibrations. The exciter lamp throws a beam of light through the lens tube, which, when concentrated, falls across the sound track.

Behind the sound track is the photo-electric cell, which is dead until the light beam from the sound track penetrates it, by means of a small condensing lens. The volume is then opened out, and after being greatly amplified, these vibrations are transferred from the box along wires to the speakers behind the screen. The screen itself is honeycombed with small holes to enable the sound to be distinctly heard all over the cinema.

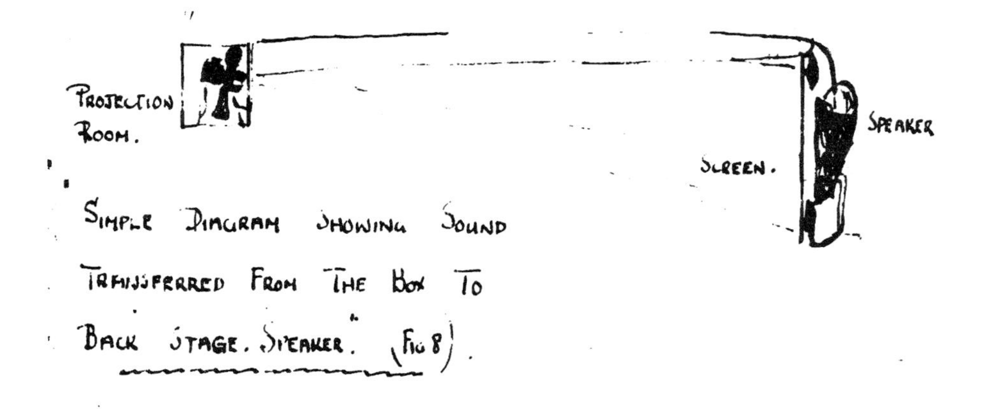

SIMPLE DIAGRAM SHOWING SOUND TRANSFERRED FROM THE BOX TO BACK STAGE. SPEAKER. (FIG 8)

The types of sound systems are many: Western Electric, B.T-H., R.C.A., Morrison, Gaumont-British Acoustic, and many others of lesser-known makes. Sound systems are not purchased outright. They are leased from the companies for a period of five or six years, at the end of which time cinema managements have the choice of renewing the contract, or having a new set installed.

Chapter III – Running The Show
(Programme preparation, breaks, maintenance)

Now, in this chapter let us journey side by side with the projectionist throughout the course of the day – the preparation and running of the show. The day is a Monday, and we arrive at the cinema about 9 o'clock in the morning. In the vestibule stand three or four large heavy boxes, these are the films. We wait; the operator takes his films up to the box.

A few moments later we follow him. Up a long stairway, at the top of it is a door marked "No Smoking", and wherever you see that sign in a cinema you can be sure you are near the 'box'. We open the door and enter and the first thing to greet us is the atmosphere. It is close, stuffy, and a pungent smell of carbon and pear drops fills the air. Taking up most of the space are the projectors: huge things, much bigger than we thought they were. They are covered up. On the floor beneath them are grimy patches of oil, and white dust which has been blown by the wind down the fume carriers. We pass through the box and enter a small room at the back. This is the re-winding room, and stacked up on the bench are the cans of film ready for winding on to the empty spools. Screwed to the bench is the rewinder: a large handle, geared up so as to maintain high speed when cranked by hand. It is on much the same principle as an emery wheel.

The operator places his first reel on the empty spindle of the rewinder. The loose end of film is pulled to the empty spool and clipped in. The handle is turned, and winding-up has commenced. As he winds, the operator holds the running film between his thumb and first finger of the left hand. By this method he can feel any broken pieces of film or bad joints. Occasionally he stops and examines the film—any doubtful parts of torn celluloid must be cut out and the film re-joined. Amyl acetate and acetone mixed together is the ideal solvent for celluloid, so on the bench stands a small bottle ready for use.

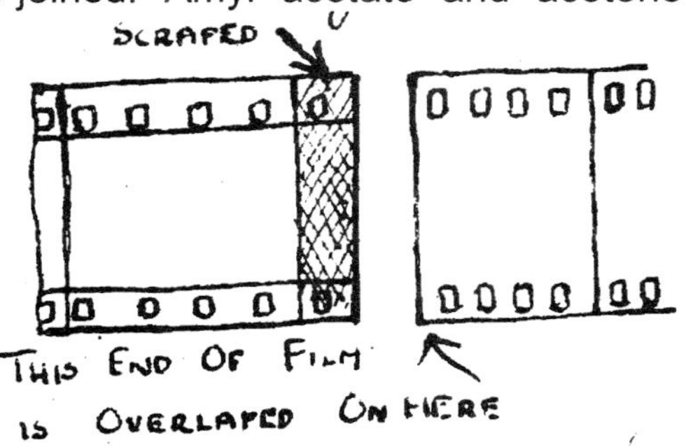

This diagram shows the film joint. One end of the film is scraped for just the space of a sprocket hole, and then the film cement is applied. The two pieces of film are then placed exactly on top of each other and pressed together for a few seconds.. This completes the joint and re-winding can proceed.

In this visit to the 'box' the feature film is *The Great Lie* in eleven reels. Each reel is wound up on a spool and placed in the fireproof compartment of the "programme bin". When the feature is finished the operator starts preparing the supporting programme, *British Movietone News*, *Pluto's Dream House* (coloured cartoon), and *The March of Time*. When finished he makes a chart for the benefit of himself and his assistants (there are three operators in this particular cinema). The chart looks like this:

PROGRAMME				**Time of showing**		
NEWS	Fox	1 reel	10 mins.	2.00	4.45	7.30
CARTOON	Radio	1 reel	10 mins.	2.10	4.55	7.40
March of Time	Radio	2 reels	20 mins.	2.20	5.05	7.50
Trailers	--	--	2 mins.	2.40	5.25	8.10
INTERVAL			3 mins.	2.42	5.27	8.12
THE GREAT LIE	Warner Bros.	11 reels	120 mins.	2.45	5.30	8.15
ANTHEM						10.15

So to the operator the programme runs like this: News – 1 reel Cartoon – 1 reel March of time & trailers – 2 reels joined on 1 spool The Great Lie – 11 reels.

Now the programme is ready to run, and that finished the operator next looks to his equipment. He uncovers his projectors then proceeds to oil them carefully. After a general check-up of the equipment he leaves for home.

At 1.30, after dinner he arrives back at the theatre. The show according to the programme is due to commence at 2 o'clock, and the projectionists always arrive half an hour before the time of showing to get ready.

First – the power is switched on. ii – the machines are switched on, so that the electric motors can sufficiently 'warm up'. iii – the sound is put on to 'warm the valves'. iv – the house lights in the cinema are raised up full, and the exit signs lit. The projectionist returns to the box, stops the machines, and threads them up. Suddenly, there is a small "buzz" – this is the manager pressing the electric buzzer to inform the 'chief' that the public is coming into the hall. The 'chief' crosses to the "Non-synchronised set" and puts on a record. The time now is almost 2 o'clock.

When he has threaded, or laced up the machines, he places fresh carbons in the arc lamps. Now everything is ready. He calls his assistants' attention (he is the Chief, the other operators are termed as the Second and Third, or film boy). "Stand by", he shouts. The Third stands by the dimmer, ready to fade out the house lights, and open the curtains by the small curtain control switch (the curtains are referred to as 'tabs'). The Second puts the main on and strikes the arc lamp up. The Chief stands by to see that everything runs to plan.

"O.K." he shouts "fade out the house." (houselights)

"Start your motor." (projector)

"Fade out the record" – over to sound

"Open your shutter, now the tabs, and now fade out the foots."

The performance has commenced. To the patrons downstairs, the houselights have gone out, the curtains have opened, and he is now watching the newsreel.

Up in the 'box', the newsreel is running through on the No. 1 machine. The Second who started the projector up has now handed it over to the Chief, who remains on it until the news has run its course. When it is almost ended he tells the Second to strike the arc of No. 2 projector. Then at the conclusion he shuts off, and his Second starts up the cartoon After it has been on for some moments the Chief takes it over, the Second carbons up the No.1 projector, the Third rewinds the newsreel, and then threads up *The March of Time*. This is the procedure all day until 10.15, when *God Save The King* is played.

At the beginning of this chapter I mentioned 'breaks and maintenance', but it is really unnecessary to say anything about it. Breaks on modern up-to-date machinery are very few and far between. As for maintenance, as long as the equipment is kept reasonably clean there should be no trouble. On the large circuits, such as A.B.C., G-B., Odeon, Granada and Paramount service engineers are employed whose duty it is to check up individual cinemas every month. The R.C.A. and Western Electric sound systems are checked up in the same way. As there isn't so much maintenance work required of the operator, as in days gone by, I shall omit it.

Illustrated Supplement of some of the Equipment used in the Projection Rooms of Today

The American Simplex Model E7
(as used at the Regal, Kettering)

This projector is closed up in a case when in motion. This is not a great success, however, for the aperture plates run too hot, making it unsafe to thread up the next reel of film until it has cooled down somewhat.

The British Ross Projector
(as used at the Savoy, Northampton 1936-c.1953)

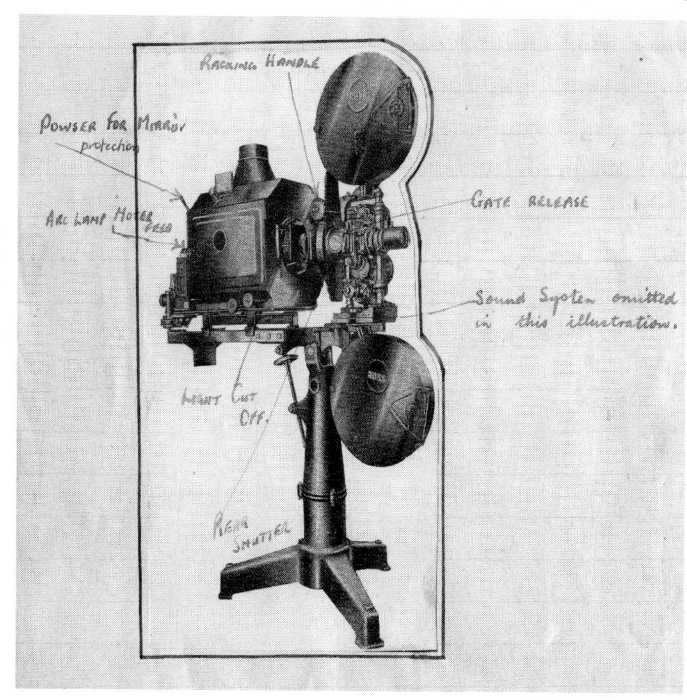

This projector is well favoured by Associated British Cinemas. It is used in almost every one of their theatres in conjunction with the Ross Searchlight arc lamp, as in the illustration.
It is a well-built heavy machine, and will withstand heavy usage. Some have run as long as ten to fifteen years, with only an occasional overhaul.

The German Ernemann projector
(as used at the Picturedrome and Cinema de Luxe cinemas, Northampton)

The illustration is of a German projection box, equipped with Ernemann projectors and Zeiss Ikon Artisol arc lamps.
One feature of this projector is the spool box size, large enough to accommodate 30mins. uninterrupted projection. Of course, this is forbidden in Great Britain owing to the danger of fire. 20mins. film in the top magazine is all that is allowed.

The Kalee 7
(as used at the Regal and Coliseum cinemas, Northampton)

This is a Kalee 7, out-of-date in most of the large cinemas of today. The latest model (1942) is the Kalee 12. This illustration is fitted with Kalee Emel L1 lamphouse and R.C.A. soundhead.

The Gaumont-British "Eclipse" projector – ex Chrono (as used at the Plaza and Exchange cinemas, Northampton)

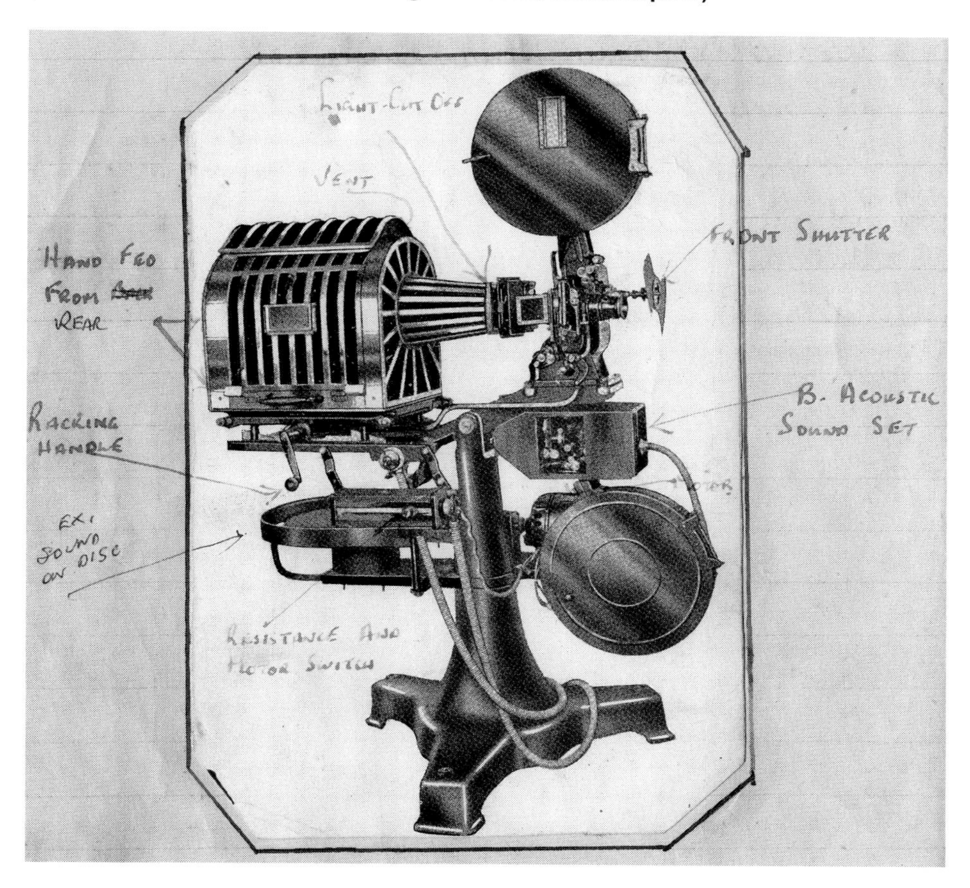

Obviously this machine is favoured by the Gaumont theatres, in conjunction with the Gaumont-British Acoustic sound system.

One of its unique features is the racking handle which is fitted to the side of the arc lamp. This device enables the arc lamp to be wound up and down in order to eliminate racks of any kind.

Most of its components were manufactured in France before the war.

Some typical cinema interiors and exteriors

The Odeon, Edgware Road, London – with B.T-H. sound

A Union Cinemas house – The Ritz exterior and interior

Postscript

Now you have read this brief explanation of cinema operating I hope you have some idea of the lines on which a cinema (large or small) is run. If you have, I shall feel as if I have at least accomplished something by writing it.

A cinema projectionist's life is such an odd one. He works all hours, receives nothing in return for it but a handful of rice, so to speak, comparing him with members of other skilled trades. Yet he never gives it up, for once anyone has manned the projectors in a large cinema, it is very rare he gives up easily. There is, I think, a certain fascination that holds one to the job.

Some people may say "Well, when you're finished work for the night, what have you got to show for it?" I would at once answer, "The satisfaction obtained is watching the audience walk out, smiling, or, half in tears. By your work in the box you have achieved this: the film, whether it was comedy or drama was sent to you in a small flat box.

The 16-year old author wrote this, in a careful hand, in a lined school exercise book. The illustrations were cut out of Trade periodicals, magazines, and catalogues and pasted in, with arrows and labels drawn in. It is here presented for the first time since it was written 60 years ago. It is a document of its time and place, and shows us details of the chain of command in a projection room – now lost through single-manning of boxes. It has been edited only very lightly, mainly for spelling, to leave intact the authentic voice of the author. His original preface, more an afterword, follows.

Preface

Now this book is finished I still don't know what induced me to write it. Perhaps I wanted to convey my experiences in the cinema to others, perhaps I wrote it just for amusement – perhaps!

It is not meant to be remarkable or unusual, just a plain explanation of cinema operating. Who runs the show, and how it's all done, is something others should know more about. Perhaps that is why I did write this story, to inform other about a man they know little, or nothing, about – the man in the box...

A. E. N

Index – illustrations in *italics*

This does not include 'Flash-backs' or 'The Man in the Box.'

MERCIA PUBLICATIONS

The **Black Family** of **Sunderland**	Frank Manders	£ 2.00
Buckinghamshire Picture Palaces	Martin Tapsell	£ 2.50
Ribbon of Dreams (**Cardiff** cinemas)	Gary Wharton	£8.85/£7.50
The **Clifton** Cinema Circuit	Brian Hornsey	£ 2.00
Temple of Dreams (**Eastbourne**)	Peter R. Hodges	£ 7.00
The **Essoldo** Circuit	Brian Hornsey	£ 3.00
Cinemas of **Essex**	Bob Grimwood	£13.50/12.00 (+£3.20p+p)
Cinemas and Theatres of **Exeter**	Stuart Smith	£ 6.00/£4.90
The Cinemas of **Halifax** and Calderdale	S. Smith/B Hornsey	£7.50/£7.00
The Cinemas of **Huddersfield** and Kirklees	S. Smith/B Hornsey	£8.50/£8.00
Cinema on the Roman Wall (**Hexham**)	Peter Douglas	£ 1.50
Cinemas of **Keighley** & the Aire Valley	Stuart Smith	£ 6.00/£4.90
Cinemas of **Lincoln**	George Clarke	£ 4.00
Loughborough's Stage & Screen (+**Coalville** & the Deeming Circuit)	Mervyn Gould	£15.50/£13.00
Cinemas of **Mexborough/Dearne Valley**	Stuart Smith	£ 7.20/£6.00
Five or More (**Multiplexes**)	Kate Taylor/B Hornsey	£ 3.00
The Dream Palaces of **Oxford**	Sean Currell	£ 3.00
Chronicles of **Pendle** Picture Palaces	Peter Sagar	£7.50/6.50
Dream Palaces of **Richmond/Thames**	Fred Windsor	£ 2.30
Rotherham Film Pioneers	Stuart Smith	£ 2.60
The Cinemas of **South Tyneside**	Doris Johnson	£ 5.80
50 Years of the **ABC Wakefield**	Kate Taylor	£ 1.40
Wakefield Cinema Story	Kate Taylor	£ 7.75/£5.50
Cinemas of North **Wales**	Brian Hornsey	£ 8.25
Remembering **Whitstable** Cinemas	Michael Glover	£6.50/£5.50
Cinemas of the Weisker Brothers	Brian Hornsey	£ 2.00
Cinemas of **York**	Peter Wren/ Kate Taylor	£ 6.90/£5.50
Researching the History of Cinemas	Kate Taylor/Nick Prince	£ 2.05

- Sales Officer **100 Wickfield Road Hackenthorpe Sheffield S12 4TT**
- double-pricing: the lower is **the discount price** available to Mercia members
- Cheques to **Mercia Cinema Society (+membership no. for discount)**
- All prices include post & packing unless otherwise stated
- Sales telephone line 0777 155 4605
- Trade enquiries welcomed